From Your Head To Your Heart

BIBLE STUDY GUIDE:

The Change You Long For Is Just 18
Inches Away

MARIA DURSO

Wow! Maria has hit the target in this much-needed book. She knows intimately the difference between the head and the heart. Our culture's tendency to try to figure out life and its challenges intellectually is facing a battle that, without this revelation from Scripture, cannot be won. You and I have to realize that our feelings will betray us at every step. We can't analyze God's forgiveness and love for us. The key is our heart. The apostle Paul tells us in Ephesians 1 that we have been blessed with every spiritual blessing. But it's hard to realize the vastness of this truth. We need to have His spirit of wisdom and revelation to fully grasp His love and have our hearts mended and healed. Only then can we walk by faith and not by sight or by feeling.

Michael and Maria Durso are both living and walking miracles. There's no denying that. Their love for Christ and for each other, and their compassion for people are what make them so attractive to others. That's why I love them and count them as dear friends.

Right on, Maria!

—Nicky Cruz
Evangelist and Author

Generally people don't like change. Maria Durso's amazing personal journey and God's intervention reveals the extraordinary transformation available to us all who dare to believe in Jesus. This is a change everyone should welcome. It's not just good for you. It's also essential for a life of joy, hope, and love. When you read this book, you will learn how to find peace with God for yourself, and how to lead others to do so. This is a change you can live for.

—Commissioner James M. Knaggs
Territorial Commander, The Salvation Army

Maria is a unique person with a life story that will bring tears and a greater faith for what the Lord can do to change a person from the worst of circumstances to a miracle of grace transformation. This book will touch the lives of all who read it. Great job, Maria!

—Frank DaMazio
Lead Pastor, City Bible Church, Portland, Oregon

It has been said that emotion is the hinge of logic. Although we are wholly intellectual and logical creatures, deep change occurs when people get to our hearts. Maria Durso is masterful at getting to our hearts because she bravely opened up her heart to God and now to us in this wonderful work.

—David D. Ireland, PhD
Senior Pastor, Christ Church, Montclair, New Jersey
Author of *The Kneeling Warrior* (www.DavidIreland.org)

I have never met anyone who loves the voice of the Lord more than Maria Durso! Maria's devotion and dedication in worship and to the Word of God are contagious. The insights and revelation Maria finds in Scripture are so full of freedom and power that it is evident her time spent with the Lord produces deep wells of wisdom. There is a trust Maria carries from the Lord for the lost and broken that is rare and priceless. Maria's passion for redemption and wholeness is a literal gift to the body of Christ everywhere!

—Rita Springer
Worship Leader and Recording Artist

From the moment I read the introduction of this book authored by my dear friend Maria Durso, I knew it would be a powerful instrument for deep healing. Many people walk through this life unaware that they have a heart condition. They feel the effects, but they can't locate the cause.

In this amazing book you will go on a journey into the depths of your heart, and the adage "my heart has a mind of its own" will come alive to you.

You will discover things buried deep that will finally surface and be removed through the revelatory information within these pages. And when you have read the last line, you will find, as Maria did, that God is able to do exceedingly and abundantly above what you could ask or think!

—Carol Kornacki
Evangelist and Author

Maria is not only gifted with insight on church and family matters. Her spiritual insight and ability to communicate God's Word in a very practical and life-changing way will also bless every reader. She is gifted to teach each person how easy it is to not only know the Lord but also to walk with Him every day.

—Mary Colbert
Cofounder of Divine Health Ministries
Author of *13 Women You Should Never Marry*

Maria Durso has written a book that offers us the possibility of actualizing success in every area of our lives. She teaches that if we get our hearts right we can get everything right. And since Scripture does, in fact, intimate that the heart feels, reasons, understands, imagines, discerns right and wrong, and makes decisions, I couldn't agree more with the message of this book. Even more than the message, though, I am struck by the credibility of the messenger. Maria absolutely embodies this truth. She and her husband, Michael—who have led one of the great churches in New York City for more than thirty years—are dear friends and mentors to me and my wife, Sharon. I can affirm that Maria is a living testimony to this powerful message.

I highly recommend Maria and her wonderful book.

—Terry A. Smith
Lead Pastor, The Life Christian Church
West Orange, New Jersey
Author of *Live 10: Jump-Start the Best Version of Your Life*

Maria Durso passionately embodies the profound message in her new book. There is, indeed, a powerful, life-altering link between the heart and the head. In her book Maria articulates with anointing God's vision to bring about a fiery fusion between the heart and the head through the empowering enablement of the Holy Spirit. Every time I hear Maria share, I find my own heart aflame and my mind challenged and changed. For everyone who dares to pick up these pages and read them, I am sure they too will experience a heart and head revolution.

—Corey Jones
Lead Pastor, Crossroads Tabernacle, Fort Worth, Texas

If there was anyone I would trust with the absolute priority of moving the knowledge of God from head to heart it would be Maria Durso. I have stood next to her in Christ Tabernacle prayer meetings and heard her passionately cry out to God for the church and community. I watched her stand for years with unmovable faith for her three sons through some dark days until they became the men of God they are today. I have heard her stir the hearts of audiences of all ages with her life story and vibrant preaching. Maria has a heart ablaze for God, and I am confident the Holy Spirit will set your heart ablaze through the pages of this book.

—Alec Rowlands, DMin
Senior Pastor, Westgate Chapel, Edmonds, Washington
President of Church Awakening, Edmonds, Washington

DEDICATION

First and foremost, this book is dedicated to none other than the Holy
Spirit. For years when people said I should write a book, I always
responded by saying, "If God wants me to write a book, He will send a
publisher to me."

When I went to write the book, I was terrified and felt I needed a
ghostwriter. The Holy Spirit clearly spoke to me and said, "You don't need
a ghostwriter. You have the Holy Ghost writer." Sure enough, He has been
the source of all these revelations.

I'd also like to dedicate this book to all those who have struggled just
like me to truly believe in the deepest recesses of their hearts that they are
loved and valued by God. May they all make the eighteen-inch journey.

TABLE OF CONTENTS

ACKNOWLEDGMENTS

Above all I want to thank my amazing and most precious husband, Michael, who for almost forty years has always been my biggest cheerleader. Thank you, Michael, for gently sitting me down and urging me not to procrastinate any longer and reminding me that I was made for this. Thank you for patiently reading the chapters—all the chapters—over and over and over again. You are my greatest love and encourager.

To my amazing sons . . .

Adam, who would have thought that the little boy who said he wanted to be president would become one of the leading influencers of this generation, changing the face of youth ministry. You have also been a prophetic voice to speak to those who have the ability to influence. You are one of the most brilliant, insightful, and sensitive people I know.

Jordan, who would have thought the little boy who would never sleep in anyone's house would end up traveling to the four corners of the earth. You not only came God's representative in presidential palaces but also brought the gospel and humanitarian aid to the least of these. You are one of the most compassionate, merciful, and fearless people I know.

Chris, who would have thought the little boy who was diagnosed with ADHD and called stupid in the first grade by his teacher would write a revolutionary book and lead one of the most impactful youth and young adult ministries in the nation. God has propelled you to stand on the most coveted platforms around the world. You are one of the most tender, creative, and loving people I know.

Each one of you is a world-changer in your own right, and I know that for a fact, because you have changed my world. I am your greatest fan! Thank you for fanning into flame the gift of God within me. I cannot even imagine what the Lord has in store for all of you and Papa and Nana's grandbabies.

To my daughters-in-law, Lucy and Yahris—God gave my sons the most well-suited and priceless gift when He gave you to them. You were tailor-made to be a perfect fit for our family and the missing pieces of my heart.

To Ralph Castillo, my son in the Lord—who would have thought when you walked into our home as a young child you would have walked into our hearts. To me, you are the poster child for this book. Although the odds were against you, you took the eighteen-inch journey and became one of the godliest men and most brilliant communicators I know.

I want to thank my incredible assistant, Penny Mack, who is worth a million to me. I could never do without you. You tirelessly helped me with my research and stood by my side, supporting me every step of the way.

I want to thank Marie Armenia, who is an amazing author in her own right. You gave me a parade—marching band and all—after every rewrite. You could have definitely finished your own book with all the time you took with this one. Thank you, my friend.

To my precious Diana Denis, I watched you grow up, and grow up you did. You are so incredibly gifted, and you encouraged me to fulfill my calling. Thank you.

To Renee Fisher, your willingness and enthusiasm to see this book in print was a godsend. What an incredible gift you are to the Body of Christ and to me.

To the Intercessory Prayer Band at Christ Tabernacle, my fellow soldiers, and their "general," Brenda Finn, who have continually blown the wind of God behind me throughout the whole eighteen-inch journey—none of this would ever be possible without all of you. Last but not least, my family at Christ Tabernacle, who together have taken the eighteen-inch journey through every season for three decades. Pastoring alongside my husband has been my greatest joy. There is no place like home. I love you, and I need you. I love my church!

FOREWORD

Maria Durso is incredibly qualified to talk about the changes Jesus can make in a life. In fact, you could say she has a PhD on the subject! Her book, *From Your Head to Your Heart*, chronicles not only the startling change God made in her own life, but also the many valuable lessons she has learned—along with the way since that memorable day when she became a walking miracle.

Much of religion in the twenty-first century focuses only on facts about God, which I hope gets stored in our brains. But when it comes to experiencing the transforming power of Jesus Christ in a way that alters everything about us, that is another story altogether. God has raised up Maria to proclaim and teach about something much deeper than mental concepts about the Creator of the universe. She invites the reader to experience real change that comes from Someone who loves us more than we can imagine.

The word *change* intimidates or frightens many today since it always seems safer to stick with the status quo. But Maria Durso's new book calms all those fears as she explains the steps that will lead us to a peace-, joy-, and purpose-filled life beyond our wildest dreams. What makes it so powerful is that it all happened in her own life. She's not an author with a mere argument or doctrinal position. She knows personally that the distance between your head and your heart holds the secret that unlocks all the beautiful things a loving God has planned for your life. Read this carefully—meditate on its simple truths—and experience the same wonderful changes that God gave to Maria.

—Jim Cymbala
Senior Pastor
Brooklyn Tabernacle

INTRODUCTION

I became a Christian in 1975. I was saved from a very reckless and sinful past. As you will read in this book, I was instantly delivered from drug abuse, partying, and an immoral lifestyle the day I walked down the long aisle in church to give my life to Christ. My external sinful behaviors were immediately gone. But what was not as immediate was being delivered from years and years of low self-esteem. It would take decades for me to feel I was truly loved and accepted by God—that *I* had value and worth, and that a holy God could possibly use someone with a past like mine. I lived my life in turmoil and private agony. A battle raged within. I knew in my mind that Jesus loved me, "for the Bible tells me so." I knew in my mind that I was not an orphan, because God's Word tells me that I've been adopted and grafted into His family. But it would be years and years before that thinking would transfer into my heart.

I always felt like there was sludge between my head and my heart. I would have to fight through layers and layers of resistance before the truth could finally be transferred into my heart. The battle was intense. I read great books about the battlefield of the mind, but knowing something in your head and knowing it in your heart are worlds apart. Being assured in your heart that you are loved is a far cry from just knowing it in your head. Trusting someone in your head and trusting someone in your heart is as different as knowing someone as an acquaintance and having that person as your best friend. Knowing in your heart is the game changer. Your heart seals the deal.

It has been said that there is a distance of eighteen inches between the head and the heart—a separation of a foot and a half. When I look back, I realize I was oftentimes just eighteen inches from victory. Only eighteen inches of steep terrain needed to be conquered. The distance of eighteen inches may seem short, but the road is extremely long and winding. Yet this distance can definitely be shortened and the road made much less turbulent when we make a vital connection.

In 1991 Dr. J. Andrew Armour introduced the idea that the heart has its own brain. In his book *Neurocardiology* Armour revealed that the heart "has an elaborate circuitry that allows it to act independently of the cranial brain—to learn, remember, even sense and feel."[1] *Ah!* This extremely important information would confirm what I had felt all these years—and prove that I wasn't a weirdo! I also realized that if this was, in fact, true, then number one, the Bible would confirm it (because science will ultimately prove what God has written in His Word). Number two, I wouldn't be the only one sensing this deep divide on the inside.

According to the research, the brain in the head is connected to the brain in the heart. The two brains send messages to each other through thousands of neurons and tiny filaments, but the messages don't necessarily coincide.[2] To us laymen this may seem to be just some boring medical information that has nothing to do with us or our spiritual life. But I assure you it has everything to do with us. This affects every facet of our lives, especially our spiritual life.

Think about the reality behind this truth. Don't we oftentimes say things like, "My mind is telling me one thing, but my heart is saying something else"? This is why our behaviors often are out of sync with what we profess to believe. No bona fide, born-again Christian would dare read the Word and say outright, "Well, I really don't believe that," or, "I think God is a liar because what I feel doesn't match up at all with what I read." *Never!* This is why many times we can hear a sermon, walk out of church believing that we can scale a wall, truly know that God's Word is yea and amen, and yet a week later find that the excitement behind that life-changing truth has fizzled out. It's as though the revelation thief stole the faith we had to live out the truth we received.

I don't think the problem was with our ability to believe the truth in our minds. I believe that as the truth was working its way down into our heart, it was suddenly rejected and expelled by the heart's brain because of some fear and past experience. We had a heart attack of sorts. The heart is the seat of our emotions, not the mind. It's where all the action in our lives takes place. The Bible says in Proverbs 23:7 that as a man *thinks in his heart, so is he.* It doesn't say as a man thinks *in his head.* Proverbs 3:5 says, "Trust in the Lord with *all your heart,* and lean not on your own understanding" (NKJV, emphasis added). It doesn't say, "Trust in the Lord with *all your head*"! The Bible clearly differentiates between the head and the heart. Psalm 26:2 says, "Examine me, O Lord, and prove me; try *my mind* and *my heart*" (NKJV, emphasis added).

Although the battle in our minds is very real, I don't think we can ignore this other battlefront that must be won in the heart. The war raging in the mind is only half the battle. The heart's brain must be healed from all the years of disappointment and rejection. We need God to heal our broken hearts—or shall we say the broken way our hearts think!

I believe we are just eighteen inches from victory, and just as a firefighter identifies the source of a fire in the midst of ruins, so can we start to identify the hotspots from where the battle rages and ask God to heal them. My prayer is that this book would be like a long-awaited prescription, and that when you finish reading these pages, healing would start to flow. I believe that after we identify these vulnerable places—these "hotspots"—God will be able to give us the "brain wash" needed to heal the hemorrhaging brain in our hearts. So let's start to take the eighteen-inch trek from our heads all the way down into the deep valley of our hearts, so we can slay the giants that are defying God's promises and blocking our blessings!

WELCOME

My prayer for you is that *From Your Head to Your Heart Bible Study Guide* will be an exciting adventure allowing God's Word to produce not only a change of mind but also a change of heart!

This study was prepared with certain goals in mind:

- To change the way you view the study of God's Word. Bible study is more than facts about God that are stored in our brains; it is the transforming power of Jesus Christ that alters everything about us.

- To come to an understanding that although your past has shaped you thus far, God alone is the one who forms you into the person He has destined you to be.

- To recognize the pain of your past is the very conduit that creates a hunger for change. The word *change* intimidates or frightens many today since it always seems safer to stick to the status quo. This study is designed to calm all those fears as it explains the steps that will lead you to peace, joy and a purpose filled life beyond your wildest dreams.

- To allow my personal life story to be an encouragement to you— that what has happened *to* you in the past does not have to be the final say in your life!

Included with the Bible Study Guide is a welcome video, which you can view on my website in which I share segments of my life story. This study has been designed for individual use as well as applying it to a Small Group.

To assist you in your study, I've included questions entitled *Thoughts from the Heart* at the end of each lesson. These exercises will hopefully challenge you to study further and apply God's Word to your personal life. In addition, I have added *Small Group Discussion Questions*, which are formulated to get your Small Group talking about the key issues in each lesson.

To benefit most from this study guide, I encourage you to consider it a spiritual journal. That's why I've included space for recording your personal thoughts and discoveries. Most importantly, I encourage you to pray that God's grace will enable you to have an open mind and heart to believe in a personal life change!

CHAPTER 1: THE GREATEST DISTORTER OF REVELATION

"The tongue has the power of life and death" (Proverbs 18:21a).

If you look back over your life I'm sure you can identify specific moments that were accompanied by specific words that shaped your thinking. Words, whether positive or negative, can affect the course of our lives. Words can write *into us* confidence or failure, they write the script long before we step onto life's stage and find ourselves acting out the drama in our lives because words precede actions.

It is a fact—a scientific fact—that words spoken to us are etched deeply into the memory of the heart's brain. Scientists have recently confirmed that the heart actually has its own brain. The heart has the capacity to think and store memory. God's Word declares that as a man thinks *in his heart*, so is he (Proverbs 23:7, KJV). In other words, the thoughts imprinted in the brain of our heart, which came from words previously spoken to us, direct the way we view life and the way we think about ourselves.

This *heart brain* is where our feelings, or our emotions, are formed. Our emotions are the place from which most of us view life. So it is safe to say that *feelings are the greatest distorter of revelation.* Our emotions oftentimes hide the truth of God's Word. So even though you want to believe what the Bible says, it's as though there is a blockage in the brain of your heart.

There are times when we say our heart is broken, when technically the brain of your heart is broken. God says in His Word that He will bind up the broken heart. As our Great Physician, the Holy Spirit wants to mend our hearts so we can function as He intended.

When I was a little girl, I was told that I didn't have a mother because *God didn't think I deserved* one! The words: *"You don't deserve"* or *"God doesn't think you deserve"* are the ones that have shaped most of my life. Those words became imprinted in the depths of my being and formed who I thought I was, and how I thought God felt about me. I would see myself sabotaging every opportunity that came my way, all because of an inner voice shouting, *"You don't deserve it!"*

I have often said that great things can happen *to you* and *for you*, but if it doesn't happen *in you*, then the way you view yourself won't change. We are led by our hearts or, rather, by the brain in our hearts.

Our entire Christian faith is based on believing that God loves us and He alone can change us from the inside out and conform us into His image and likeness. That's the good news of the Gospel. Without this belief system being firmly fixed in place, our foundation is very shaky. The slightest hint of someone's disapproval will leave us living in fear that God is displeased with us. This fear can become crippling and will affect our relationship and service to Him because of a profound fear of failure. Nothing you do will ever seem good enough so you spend all of your time trying to gain God's approval rather than resting in the knowledge that you already have His approval because of what Christ gained for us on the Cross.

A PROFOUND REVELATION

One day while preparing to speak at a Women's Conference at Brooklyn Tabernacle, I heard God ask me a question that changed my life. The Holy Spirit asked me, *"Maria, do you believe that I really love you?"*

I thought about it for a quick second and started to weep profusely. Oh, I believed He loved others, but *me?* I had to admit to myself that I didn't believe Jesus really loved me. I knew *in my head* that He loved me, but I realized that I truly didn't believe *in my heart* that He loved me. I was eighteen inches—a foot and a half—from victory.

This was where my deep issues had their root, from where all my trust issues stemmed. The Holy Spirit neatly wrapped up every feeling of insecurity, worthlessness, and fear in an instant and narrowed it down for me by identifying my double-mindedness. The belief that God loves us is the critical truth on which the rest of our faith hinges. The failure to believe this is the difference between living our life trying to gain God's approval and living our life knowing that we already have His approval.

When we don't believe we are loved—in our hearts—we never feel like we've done enough or that we're good enough. There is no rest, no enjoyment of God's presence. We definitely need our hearts to experience a brain-wash to cleanse away all the false impressions of God.

Knowing and believing in our heart that Jesus is our defender not our accuser is the truth that sets us free! (See: The example in the life of Mary of Bethany on the next page.)

Read Luke 10:38-42. Who were Mary's accusers? Who was her defender?

Accuser - Mary (Sister)
Defender - Jesus

Read John 12:1-8. Who was Mary's accuser? Who was her defender?

Accuser - Judas Iscariot
Defender - Jesus

Read Mark 14:3-9. Who was Mary's accuser? Who was her defender?

Accuser - Disciples
Defender - Jesus

It was only when Mary saw Jesus as her defender and not her accuser that she was able to trust Him and surrender her most valued possession!

LET'S PRAY!
Let's ask God for the grace to see that He is our defender. Make your prayer personal.

Holy Spirit, reveal to me that You are my defender, not my accuser. As You reveal this truth to me, please start to wash my heart and lift all the residue of the past. I believe that as I absorb the depth of this heart-healing truth, I will make progress, and the distance between my head and heart will definitely be shortened. In Jesus' name, Amen!

THOUGHTS FROM THE HEART:

Everyone has had painful words spoken to them, some words have bounced off and others have stuck to leave a lasting impression. What has been spoken to you that stuck and shaped how you see yourself?

- My family has set the precendent of who we are, so I won't get out of that.
- Not visually the right look for ministry
- Too poor

Write in your own words why *feelings are the greatest distorter to revelation.*

Feelings dominate even the things you know to be true. They are the biggest distorter of revelation because its so easy to allow them to control your mind. Its hard to overpower your own thoughts.

Now that you are aware that your heart has a brain, express in your own words what Solomon meant in Proverbs 4:23, *"Above all else, guard your heart for everything you do flows from it."*

Who you are and what you think of yourself, is so much reflected by your heart, that we need to protect that. Guard it with the truth.

What are some of the spiritual effects of being double-minded? Read James 1:2-8 and write in your own words what James says about being double-minded.

You will not receive from the Lord. You will be tossed around by life. You will not be stable in Him, it will cause doubt.

SMALL GROUP DISCUSSION QUESTIONS:

Would you describe yourself as a confident person or someone that lives with a fear of failure? Why do you see yourself in that way?

_____

_____

_____

_____

_____

_____

Discuss how our emotions affect our belief system.

_____

_____

_____

_____

_____

_____

_____

_____

_____

Discuss with your group how you can believe God loves others yet still find it hard to believe God loves you! Is that blockage a head issue or a heart issue?

_____

_____

_____

_____

_____

_____

How do you see Jesus, is He your accuser or your defender? Can you describe what took place in your own life that caused you to have that view of Him? How has your view of Jesus affected your spiritual walk?

_____

_____

_____

_____

_____

_____

_____

_____

_____

THOUGHTS:

THOUGHTS:

_____

_____

_____

_____

_____

_____

_____

_____

_____

_____

_____

_____

_____

_____

_____

_____

_____

THOUGHTS:

CHAPTER 2: WE NEED A BRAIN WASH

"We seemed like grasshoppers in our own eyes, and we looked the same to them"
(Numbers 13:33b).

Let's go back for a moment to the mind-blowing scientific find that the heart has its own brain. Now that we know the heart has the ability to think, it stands to reason that the heart's brain has a memory bank. The heart is more than an organ that pumps blood; it also pumps past memories into our everyday life. Years of emotional data are locked up in the heart, and that is what makes it difficult to believe something that is contrary to your own personal experience. If you have been told something your whole life, even though it wasn't true, you are most likely to rely on what you have been told over and over again. So it stands to reason that for a thorough transformation we need both of our brains to be washed by God's Word so they can be in sync with His will.[1]

I believe that's what happened to the Israelites who went to scout out the land in Numbers chapter 13. They received the word from God, and went in to check out the Promised Land. The very reason they were brought out of Egypt was to be brought into the land of promise, and to fulfill their destiny!

Isn't that the reason God brought us out of the slavery of this world to bring us into a new land? They sent in their toughest and brightest, the Navy SEALS of their day, and came back with fruit so huge they had to carry it on their shoulders. This was concrete proof that what God said was true. They confirmed that the land absolutely did flow with milk and honey, and there was no record of anyone chasing them. No one in the land seemed to have any beef with them. As a matter of fact, Rahab the prostitute said, *"I know that the Lord has given you this land and that a great fear of you has fallen on us"* (Joshua 2:9a).

Yet they came back with fruit in hand and fear in their hearts. Fear so enveloped them that they were sure God was setting them up to fail. They acknowledged the fruit was huge and the land was fertile, but they said the people were like giants and the land was too large to conquer. Then they declared, *"We seemed like grasshoppers in our own eyes, and we looked the same to them."*

The Israelite enemy wasn't on the outside it was on the inside. It wasn't the giants in the land that threatened to defeat them it was the giants of low self-esteem and low self-worth within them. All their lives they were the underdogs so it stands to reason that their past was present with them. What they knew to be true in their heads and what they saw with their own eyes couldn't stand up to what they felt in their hearts. The Israelites were only 18 inches from victory—*so close but yet so far!* It's amazing that how we see ourselves is the way we think everybody sees us, and the way we feel becomes our reality. The question I have for you is, *"Do you see yourself with a grasshopper mentality?"*

Allow me to give you some interesting grasshopper facts:

- *Grasshoppers* travel in large numbers but have absolutely no purpose. Because they travel in such large numbers they obscure the sun and hide the light.
- *Grasshoppers* are destructive; they ravage the land without replenishing it or contributing to it in any way.
- *Grasshoppers* have an unusual habit of eating one another instead of eating other insects. In other words, they eat their own kind.
- *Grasshoppers* are the chief target or prey of other insects and reptiles.
- *Grasshoppers* when attacked, instead of fighting back by using their strong jaws to bite or their amazing ability to jump onto higher ground—they usually exhibit no movement at all. They blend into their surroundings, frozen in fear.[2]
- All types of filthy flies, full of bacteria, lay their eggs and hatch their young on the backs of grasshoppers. The baby flies eat their way through the eggshell, eating the grasshopper alive in the process, and the grasshopper just sits there and allows it to happen.[3]

Can you see the typology in this? When we have a grasshopper mentality we can display many of these traits. Take some time and use your imagination and write down how these traits can play out in your life.

_____

_____

_____

_____

_____

_____

_____

In the book, I shared a story about the leaky *old* pipes in my house, when we are born again we are given new life—new pipes, if you will! Didn't God say, *"I will give you a new heart and put a new spirit in you"* (Ezekiel 36:26a)?

In verse 25, just one verse up, God explains how this process will take place. Write out what God says He will do and describe in your own words what you think the clean water represents.

_____

_____

_____

_____

_____

_____

_____

_____

_____

_____

God promises to wash us clean. His Word is able to remove all the sludge and gunk of the past. We *must* come to terms with the fact that its to our benefit to *"get into the Word"* so that the Word can *"get into us"*—every part of us. But when those cleansing waters are met with opposition, i.e., the sludge of our thinking—a wall of impenetrable cement that resists God's Word, our heart's brain—our old way of thinking—becomes a blockage to our freedom!

Our emotions have had the run of the house for all these years, and they don't like the new connection, especially since it involves change on our part. This change requires the willingness to trust God, believe His promises and obey His Word. Trust and obey for there is no other way! If not we will keep going around the same old mountain, fighting the same old enemies.

WHO ARE YOU REALLY?

"Let the Word of Christ ... have the run of the house" (Colossians 3:16, MSG).

So who are you, and what are you thinking? Whatever you think in your heart is who you really are. That's why the brain in the heart, along with the brain in your head needs a continual spiritual Roto-Rooter—an eighteen-inch brain wash from top to bottom. God's Word should be running rampant throughout all the cracks and crevices of our *"house"* which is our inner man. God's Word *must* win this tug-of-war and bring down the proponent of oppositional thinking. As God's Word continually soaks us, it will soften us, making supple and pliable all those rock-hard, resistant places. Then the Lord will be able to write on the tablets of our heart what He truly thinks about us.

All too often we give people and their opinions power and allow them to define us instead of God's Word. We allow things to cripple us, things past and present that can blind us to God's plan for our lives. In Ephesians 1:18 the apostle Paul prayed this profound prayer of revelation:

"I pray that the eyes of your heart may be enlightened in order that you may know the hope to which he has called you, the richest of his glorious inheritance in his holy people."

Your heart not only has a brain, but it also has eyes—eyes that need to be enlightened so that you will be able to see the hope to which you were called. It's only then that we can see who we really are in Christ! Paul goes on in verses 19-22 that we might know, *"his incomparably great power for us who believe."*

We cannot allow the enemy to keep us from believing we must allow God's Word to give us that incomparable power that belongs to those who believe!

LET'S PRAY!

Holy Spirit, please open the eyes of my heart so that I would truly gain understanding and a new depth of insight to know who You are and who I am in You. Clean my heart with Your Word, from all those negative opinions that I've allowed to define me. Cause me to allow Your Word to have the run of my house. I thank You that I am truly able to love You because You loved me first. Thank You that I am already on the road to victory because of the power that lives in me. In Jesus' name, Amen!

THOUGHTS FROM THE HEART:

Out of all the facts listed about grasshoppers which one can you more readily identify with?

_____

_____

_____

_____

_____

_____

Philippians 4:13 states, *"I can do all this through him who gives me strength."* Do you see this verse operating in you life or is it just a memory verse in your head but not in your heart? Explain:

_____

_____

_____

_____

_____

_____

_____

_____

_____

Write out Proverbs 3:5-6 then in your own words explain the key component to this verse.

_____

_____

_____

_____

_____

I shared a testimony of how the opinion of others crippled me for so many years. What things have crippled you? What things from your past are still present with you?

_____

_____

_____

_____

_____

_____

_____

_____

_____

_____

SMALL GROUP DISCUSSION QUESTIONS:

Read Numbers Chapter 13 and discuss how what the Israelite scouts saw with their own eyes differed from what they believed and how it affected their report.

_____

_____

_____

_____

_____

What was the difference between the 10 scouts that gave a negative report and the report that Joshua and Caleb gave? Why did the two reports differ so much?

_____

_____

_____

_____

_____

_____

_____

_____

_____

What happens when the cleansing water of God's Word is met with opposition? What is necessary to break that cement wall of opposition that blocks our way to freedom?

_____

_____

_____

_____

_____

_____

_____

_____

_____

_____

_____

_____

_____

_____

_____

_____

THOUGHTS:

THOUGHTS:

_____

_____

_____

_____

_____

_____

_____

_____

_____

_____

_____

_____

_____

_____

_____

_____

_____

CHAPTER 3: ASHES, ASHES

"Carry the ashes outside the camp to a place that is ceremonially clean" (Leviticus 6:11).

The Book of Leviticus was heaven's sacred recipe book, filled with ways to cook up different types of worship meals for different seasons. There were different requirements, or *recipes*, for each feast day, Day of Atonement, or day of grief. It was like a family's traditional recipe book. There were clearly different meals for different feasts.

In my husband's family there was never any meat on Christmas Eve. Different types of seafood were plentiful; shrimp, calamari, clams, all prepared in a sauce or fried with breadcrumbs. Along with the seafood there's always pasta, of course. But there was *never* any red meat or poultry.

On Christmas day, however, everything changed. Different recipes for different days, and you could never mix them. On Christmas Day Grandma prepared her once-a-year traditional meat sauce that simmered on the stove for a minimum of six hours. There were always a variety of meats, which had to be placed into a massive pot at different intervals. You *could never* leave out one of those meats. Without the meat sauce it just wouldn't be Christmas.

But no matter how magnificent the Christmas feast turned out, everyone looked forward to Easter. No meatballs on Easter that would be a sacrilege. It was leg of lamb. And there was a whole different code for the spread prepared for a funeral. Different requirements for different occasions!

The traditional recipes for worship spoken of in the Book of Leviticus had to be followed perfectly, each according to the code of heaven. No shortcuts! Of course, we don't offer sin offerings any longer because Jesus died once and for all for our sins. We don't have fellowship offerings per se, because now we can have fellowship with the Lord any time, all the time.

The one offering that has so much typology that still can be applied to our everyday life is the burnt (consumed) offering. In Leviticus 6:8-13 we find a recipe for the priests to come before the Lord for no other reason than to have alone time with God. This offering was for pure worship and intimacy, and the recipe explained the proper way to come into His presence.

The burnt offering was a foreshadowing of Jesus Christ, the Lamb of God slain to make it possible for us to have fellowship and intimacy with God. Although the Lamb is slain, the burnt offering hasn't been done away with; it's just done in a different form. As believers in Jesus we are priest of the Lord (1 Peter 2:5; Revelation 1:6; 5:10), and our lives are to be offered up as living sacrifices to God, holy and pleasing to Him (Romans 12:1). So the sacrifice is now *alive*, and the death we as priest die is to our flesh and our will, which is absolutely a daily, ongoing thing.

The burnt offering was different from any other offering or priestly duty. Every other offering was made on behalf of the people—it was for others. But the consumed offering was for God and God alone, an offering the priest made on behalf of himself. The Bible says this particular offering was a sweet smelling aroma to God. The fragrance of this offering traveled all the way to the nostrils of God. It was sending an SOS signal to heaven, and what God saw was: *They love Me. They need Me!*

This offering is similar to our time of devotion in the mornings and evenings—an uninterrupted time set aside to pour out our hearts before God. The Lord loves when we take time out to just love Him and ask what He thinks we should do or not do.

Realize this: everything else the priests did was for someone else. But they had their own issues, burdens and regrets. Knowing this, God instituted this offering because He wanted the priests naked, spilled out, and raw—nothing hidden! We are no different. Most of what we do in life is for other people, and realistically we really can't keep on helping others unless we get alone in God's presence and spend time in His Word and in prayer.

Thank God we don't have to find a lamb, slit its neck, take the insides out, wash the organs, cut off the head and legs, trim the fat, and then place it perfectly in the line of fire, wait for the ashes to die down, change our clothes to go and throw the ashes on the ash heap, come back to the camp, change back into our priestly garments, and start all over! Thank you Jesus, we don't have to do that today.

But we do have to come naked and vulnerable before Him. We do need to take out our inward parts and allow Him to wash them in His Word. We do have to consecrate ourselves every day—our eyes, ears, mouths, and legs—so He can direct our paths. And we must place ourselves in the line of fire so God can consume our issues! So if I could sum up this way of life, it would basically be this: in order for there to be a public declaration, there must first be a private communion and conversation. Let me add that the fire on this altar also was different. God Himself came down and ignited the fire (Leviticus 9:24), but it was up to the priest to keep it burning as stated in Leviticus 6:12, *"The fire on the altar must be kept burning; it must not go out."*

We are the keepers of the fire. The fire had to be kept burning because an altar without fire doesn't please God. When the fire on the altar of our hearts grows cold, the first thing to go is intimacy, our private time with the Lord, but we continue on in our Christian duties, growing stale and losing our effectiveness. (See: Matthew 5:13-16.)

APPLYING THIS TO OUR LIVES TODAY

These were the requirements for the burnt offering describe in Exodus 29 and Leviticus 1 and the comparison to how we should live our lives with New Testament principles:

OLD

- They had to take a live lamb – no dead sacrifices.
- The lamb had to be unblemished.
- Its skin had to be peeled back.
- Its neck had to be slit.
- Its organs had to be taken out and washed.
- Its head had to be cut off.
- Its legs had to be cut off.
- The fat had to be trimmed.
- Every piece had to be arranged in the line of fire on the altar.

NEW

- Whatever we offer to God must be alive.
- Our sacrifice must be holy in appearance.
- God is concerned about our public & private life.
- We are to be laid bare before God nothing hidden.
- He desires truth in the inward parts.
- We must bring our thought life before the Lord.
- We must allow the Holy Spirit to control our steps.
- All of our accomplishments are laid on the altar.
- Sin, failure, regrets all have to go up in smoke, no longer recognizable

THE ASH HEAP

As a last step, when the priests put down his trumpet, he had to change his garment so as not to soil it. He then had to put on a different set of clothes and immediately clean away *all* the ashes on the altar and carry them outside the camp (Leviticus 6:8-12). Then, once outside the camp, he had to throw them onto the *ash heap*. This was something the priest had to do himself no one else could carry the ashes for him. Doing this was like cleaning up a crime scene so there would be no evidence left that there was anything dead on the altar—it would appear that it had always been a clean area to worship the Lord. When the priest came back into the camp, he was to change his clothes again and on a clean altar was a fresh sacrifice.

Think about the typology or symbolism of the ash heap. It was a visible reminder that all the sins and situations of the day were given to God, then and only then could they have the opportunity to start all over again with a brand new time of worship. God knew that everyone needs a brand new start.

The ashes had to be removed because they hinder the fire from burning brightly and weigh the fire down. Ashes on the altar are an insult to the one receiving the offering. It would be like trying to cook a fresh meal for a king with yesterday's soot—yesterday's failures, regrets, confessed sin, disappointments, and even our accomplishments. Instead of a vibrant altar life with fresh consecration, we start to live a dark life full of condemnation, fear and secrecy. We end up trading the altar for a closed urn where the ashes of the dead are placed, the remains of something that has passed away. The ashes become sacred and untouchable. We end up memorializing our past. We become nothing more than decorated religious jars stuck in the past.

Allow me to give you some facts about urns:

- *Urns are fireproof* – the fresh fire of God cannot penetrate.
- *Urns are waterproof* – the water of God's Word can't wash us.
- *Urns are airtight* – the breath of God cannot revive us.
- *Urns are heavy* – living in the past is a heavy weight to carry around.

Don't you think it's time we take an eighteen-inch walk to the **ash heap** and leave all our regrets and failures there? Isn't it time to open the vault of your heart where all the secrets of your past are locked up, take the lid off, and allow the light of God's presence to shine deep down inside, and then allow His wonderful loving voice to drown out the tired rhetoric of the past? We cannot walk forward while looking backwards! Give the past to the Lord, and ask Him to wash away all the sludge that keeps you from taking a giant leap forward! Isaiah 61:3 says that God will give us beauty for ashes, a garment of praise instead of a garment of heaviness!

LET'S PRAY!

Lord, I don't want to be a decorated religious jar. I don't want to live my life on a shelf. I want to be a living sacrifice, holy and pleasing to you (Romans 12:1-2). I think today is as good a day as any to bust out of my past, open the lid of the urn, and make a break for it—a prison break, that is! There's absolutely no reason for me to remain a prisoner of war in a battle that's already been won for me. I understand in my heart that there has been a changing of the guards, so I choose today to remove the weighty urn that sits front and center on the mantel of my heart, and replace it with the fresh fire of worship so that I may burn brightly for Your glory! In Jesus' name, Amen!

THOUGHTS FROM THE HEART:

Read 1 Peter 2:5 (NIV) and explain why Peter states that we are living stones? What is required for our spiritual sacrifices to be acceptable to God?

Read Exodus 29:39 and describe when the offering was to be placed on the altar. Why do you think God required the offering to be made twice a day?

In Matthew 5:13-16, Jesus uses the analogy of salt and light as a description of how effective our lives should be to others. Why do you think he used that analogy and what would cause us to loose our effectiveness?

_____

_____

_____

_____

_____

_____

I gave the requirements for the burnt offering from the Old Testament and how it relates to us in the New Testament. List in your own words how this plays out in your personal devotional time with the Lord.

_____

_____

_____

_____

_____

_____

_____

_____

SMALL GROUP DISCUSSION QUESTIONS:

The *ash heap* was a visible reminder that all the sins and situations of the day were given to God. The ashes had to be immediately removed from the altar of worship because only then could they have the opportunity to start all over again with a brand new time of worship. Discuss with your group how that applies to our everyday lives as Christians.

_____

_____

_____

_____

_____

_____

Leaving the ashes on the altar would be like rehashing the past. It wouldn't matter if the next sacrifice was unblemished and neatly laid on the altar as God instructed—the offering would be *unacceptable!* The integrity and purity of the fire would be compromised. Ashes hinder the fire from burning brightly and weigh the fire down. Discuss with your group how rehashing our past sins, regrets and failures hinder our worship.

_____

_____

_____

_____

_____

_____

_____

When we hold on to our old ashes, we unintentionally protect the ashes and neglect the fire! The ashes become sacred and untouchable and we end up memorializing our past. We dress the ashes in a beautiful decorative jar and we become nothing more than decorated religious jars, stuck in the past. Looking over the information given about urns discuss with your group how important it is to let the past go!

_____

_____

_____

_____

_____

_____

Read Romans 6:17 notice the transaction from being a slave to sin to a slave to righteousness, no longer under the law but under the covenant of grace. This change must take place in the heart! Herein lies the journey from our head to our heart. Discuss the importance of living within this pattern of grace in our life of worship.

_____

_____

_____

_____

_____

_____

_____

_____

THOUGHTS:

_____

_____

_____

_____

_____

_____

_____

_____

_____

_____

_____

_____

_____

_____

_____

_____

_____

_____

THOUGHTS:

CHAPTER 4: KEEP THAT FIRE BURNING

"The fire must be kept burning on the altar continuously; it must not go out"
(Leviticus 6:13).

Throughout the Old and New Testaments God always compares Himself to fire. On Mt. Sinai He shows up in the form of a burning bush (Exodus 13:21), the Book of Hebrews tells us that our God is a consuming fire (Hebrews 12:29); these are only two of many references throughout the Bible. So I would venture to say that God wants His people on fire, burning hot for Him!

The two trademarks of every born-again believer are the Holy Spirit, which symbolizes power; and fire, which symbolizes our passion to use the power. We are changed by His power, because of the indwelling of the Holy Spirit our lives are transformed from the inside out (Matthew 3:11).

WHY FIRE?

Why do you think God would use the symbol of fire throughout Scripture? I believe it's because there are certain properties of fire that God wants to be evident in our everyday lives.

- *Fire illuminates—it lights our pathway.* People on fire hear the still small voice within saying, *"This is the way, walk ye in it"* (Isaiah 30:21, KJV).
- *Fire melts.* Fire changes the property of even the most hardened surface; and the fire of God softens our hard hearts and makes it pliable.
- *Fire sterilizes.* I believe the Holy Spirit uses the fiery circumstances in our lives to expose and deal with the things that remain hidden—things that we learned to live with but that can cause great harm.
- *Fire radiates—it sets the temperature in the room.* The temperature is always changed by the presence of fire. The fire of the Holy Spirit is the chief source of heat in our lives and should heat every cold place we come in contact with.
- *Fire is contagious—it burns everything in its pathway.* God has created us to be spiritually combustible, human torches affecting everyone in our path.
- *Fire also has a unique ability to clear away debris that hinders new life from growing.* There is debris from our past that God wants to clear away so that new life can begin to take root in our lives and allow us to grow into the image of His Son.

HOT FOR GOD

Remember this: *God doesn't only judge our faithfulness He also judges our temperature!* Another thing that must remain *hot for God* is our gifts. Paul told Timothy to fan into flame the gift of God within Him (See: 2 Timothy 1:6-7). The implication is that the gift inside can remain dormant if we don't fan the flame.

The solution to every difficult situation in this world is the gift of God that is within every single believer. The Holy Spirit has deposited inside of every believer gifts to be used for the furtherance of God's kingdom here on earth.

Let us fan into flame every gift that God has given to us and not allow anything to put out our fire! Don't allow anything to get you to simmer down. Don't listen to the lies of the enemy that reminds you of your past and discourages you from fulfilling your future. And most importantly, don't neglect your fire, allowing devotions to be turned into duty! It's a known fact that the nature of a fire is to automatically go out! Tend to the fire in your heart and allow the Holy Spirit to continually breathe on you so that you are *hot* for God!

LET'S PRAY!

Lord, set me on fire. Consume me through and through. Every gift that You have placed in me, gifts that may be lying dormant, bring them to the boiling point. Let me be a bright light set ablaze affecting this dark world. In Jesus' name, Amen!

THOUGHTS FROM THE HEART:

Leviticus 6:12a states, *"The fire on the altar must be kept burning; it must not go out. Every morning the priest is to add firewood…"* Describe in your own words what the firewood represents and why it is important to add it in the morning.

_____

_____

_____

_____

_____

Describe in your own words why you think God uses the symbol of fire throughout the Scriptures. List three Scripture references that use the symbol of fire.

_____

_____

_____

_____

_____

_____

_____

SMALL GROUP DISCUSSION QUESTIONS:

Read 1 Timothy 4:12-16 and take some time to meditate on Paul's instructions to Timothy. In these verses Paul is exhorting us in how to keep our fire burning on the altar of our hearts so that we can have a positive affect on others. Discuss with your group the following statements:

- Don't let anyone look down on you because of your youth.
- Set an example for believers in speech, in life, in love, in faith and in purity.
- Devote yourself to the public reading of Scripture.
- Do not neglect your gift.
- Be diligent in these matters.
- How do these instructions keep our fire burning?

_____

_____

_____

_____

_____

Discuss with your group the results of following these instructions as indicated in 1 Timothy 4:15-16. Give an example from your own life how your fire for God has had an affect on others.

_____

_____

_____

_____

_____

_____

THOUGHTS:

_____

_____

_____

_____

_____

_____

_____

_____

_____

_____

_____

_____

_____

_____

_____

_____

_____

_____

THOUGHTS:

_____

_____

_____

_____

_____

_____

_____

_____

_____

_____

_____

_____

_____

_____

_____

_____

_____

CHAPTER 5: DOES *FAVOR* MEAN *FAVORITE?*

"Greetings, you who are highly favored! The Lord is with you" (Luke 1:28).

Most of us have distorted views about who God really is, whom He could possibly use, how He acts or reacts, and what certain concepts in His Word really mean. Because of these misconceptions, our Christian lives are relatively joyless, and we get bent out of shape trying to accept the very things that are supposed to be blessings. Let's try to put a small dent into some of these distortions.

Let's start with this example: Between the Old and New Testaments there is a span of four hundred years. The Book of Malachi doesn't exactly end on a high note, man is estranged from God, many priests are corrupt, and the Lord says a "day of fire" is coming. Then there is deafening silence from God!

Then the New Testament begins and God finally speaks. What do you think He would say and what would His tone be? Would He be disgusted and issue a scathing rebuke? Would He pull out a rap sheet listing all the offenses committed or go on a tirade about how disappointed He is with mankind? After all those years, whom do you think He would speak to?

God always defies human logic. He never reacts the way we think our actions would warrant, and He uses the most unlikely candidate to speak to, a teenage GIRL! God ended four hundred years of hopelessness with a divine visitation in the form of a greeting to a young girl by sending the angel Gabriel to her and saying, *"Greetings, you who are highly favored! The Lord is with you" (Luke 1:28).*

Look at Mary's response in Luke 1:29, the Bible says, *"Mary was greatly troubled at his words and wondered what kind of greeting this might be."* In other words, Mary was skeptical and probably thinking, *"Me, highly favored?"*

The word translated "troubled" in Luke 1:29 is such a strong and intensive verb, it is not used anywhere else in Scripture. It has the connotation of being greatly agitated or upset. Mary was in turmoil, I'm sure she thought that favor was for the elite group of society not an unknown girl from a poor town like Nazareth. But favor has nothing to do with your place in society, where you live, or whom you marry. According to human standards Mary's life was far from being elite or perfect. Regardless of her initial reaction to all that Gabriel had to share with Mary regarding what was about to take place she humbly accepted the challenge by responding, *"I am the Lord's servant," Mary answered, "May your word to me be fulfilled." Then the angel left her (Luke 1:38).*

FAVORED YET GOING THROUGH TRIALS

You would think that "being highly favored" would mean that everything would go well with Mary, but that couldn't be further from the truth. It was one trial after another. You can read in the Gospel of Luke the account of all that Mary went through before and during the birth of Jesus.

So it is with each of us, our trials are not an indication of whether we are favored by God or not. And sometimes the hardest trials are those that affect people that we love. In Luke 2:34-35 while in the temple for the time of purification, Simeon gives Mary a word,

"This child is destined to cause the falling and rising of many in Israel, and to be a sign that will be spoken against, so that the thoughts of many hearts will be revealed. And a sword will pierce your own soul."

Major bitterness could have set in Mary's heart after hearing that a sword, a bitter cup, a trial was coming that would pierce her *heart*. She had experienced a lot of disappointment since she said *yes* to God's will, and now these painful words were spoken to her through the mouth of a prophet. Her heart was going to be attacked, her child was going to be misunderstood and rejected. But Mary didn't become bitter, the Bible says in Luke 2:51 that Mary "treasured all these things in her heart!" Because of the condition of her heart, Jesus grew in wisdom and stature, and in favor with God and man (v. 52).

BLESSED ARE THE PURE IN HEART

Since Mary was able to keep her heart pure it served as a treasure chest that enabled her to see God in every circumstance. Matthew 5:8 says, *"Blessed are the pure in heart, for they shall see God."*

Mary understood what the term *blessed* really meant, so there was *no room* in any part of her heart for the enemy or any divisive, discouraging thought to enter in and *"cause trouble and defile many"* (Hebrews 12:15).

According to the Bible's description "favored people" experience humiliations, inconveniences and painful trials that will pierce their hearts. Too often we allow our circumstances to put us on an emotional roller coaster, one day we can think God is angry with us, and the next feel highly favored.

American Christianity has done a great disservice to us when we bring our Western ideas to the text and we sadly misinterpret what God's favor truly is. The word *favor* in Luke 1:28 is used in only one other place in Scripture Ephesians 1:6: *"Now all praise to God for his wonderful kindness to us and his **favor** that he has poured out upon us because we belong to his dearly loved Son (TLB)."*

The word *favor* in this context means "freely accepted." Favor is simply the undeserved, unearned, unmerited *grace of God* giving us what we never could have earned ourselves—not even on our best day. Grace allows the one who was unacceptable to become acceptable in His presence "just because" of divine intervention. Grace puts us in the will before we were in the family. Prior to our life beginning, God made a decision to love us through thick and thin; through the good, bad and the ugly. In Him we have forgiveness of sins, from the womb to the tomb! That is *favor*!

Because of this favor we have actually been placed inside of Christ. He covers us. He overshadows us just as the Holy Spirit overshadowed Mary. That doesn't mean our life will be perfect, but it does mean that He who began this good work in us will complete it in us (Philippians 1:6). He will work out all the kinks as we surrender our lives to Him. But first and foremost we must *accept* being *accepted!*

THE HAIL MARY "SIN-DROME"

We are greatly troubled when it comes to accepting favor because we suffer from the "Hail Mary Sin-Drome." We conclude that since we are not special and pure like she was that we are not someone the Holy Spirit would want to fill and therefore are not favored. We can see the infilling of the Holy Spirit as the reward for reaching an unattainable goal.

I believe the fact that God used a virgin shows us that there is no other way to become filled with the life of God except by the overshadowing of the Holy Spirit. That which was *in her* was not *from her*—it was divine, unexplainable, and unattainable. Could it be that the "virgin womb" was just a prototype of a clean slate. The only way we can do anything for God is by the overshadowing of the Holy Spirit!

Our response to favor should be the same as Mary's, *"May your word to me be fulfilled"* (Luke 1:38).

We must accept being accepted and highly favored. If we don't accept this basic fundamental truth we will remain spiritually impoverished and bankrupt. The more we realize that we are accepted by God the more we will walk in victory no matter what challenges we might face.

So I think it's fair to say that we might need a washing of the brain of the heart that has been clogged with wrong thinking. Let's get what we know in our heads eighteen inches down into our hearts. Let's ask the Lord to help us remove all those distortions, stereotypes, false beliefs, legalistic attitudes, and every accusation that tells us we are not good enough!

LET'S PRAY

Lord, Your Word clearly instructs us to trust in the Lord with all our hearts; so I will do as it says. I'm not going to put my trust in my circumstances, past or present, nor go by what I see. Instead I am going to put all my trust in You, and You will make every crooked path straight as I acknowledge You and Your Word in all my ways for all of my days! In Jesus' name, Amen!

THOUGHTS FROM THE HEART:

Read Luke 1:26-28 and list everything these two verses tell us about Mary.

_____

_____

_____

_____

_____

Read Luke 1:29-38 and notice the dialog between the angel and Mary. Write out the succession of Mary's response to the angel's report of what was about to take place. Her initial response verses her conclusion. What does that tell you about Mary?

_____

_____

_____

_____

_____

Read Luke 1:39-45 how did God confirm to Mary that she was truly carrying the Son of God?

_____

_____

_____

_____

_____

_____

Write out in your own words the difference between _believing in God_ and _believing God._

_____

_____

_____

_____

_____

_____

Write out Luke 1:45 and describe the importance of this affirmation in your own life.

_____

_____

_____

_____

_____

_____

_____

_____

SMALL GROUP DISCUSSION QUESTIONS:

God always defies human logic. He never reacts the why we think our actions would warrant. Discuss in your group how important it is to realize that God's thoughts and ways toward us are so different from the way we think about ourselves.

_____

_____

_____

_____

_____

You would think that "being highly favored" would mean that everything would go well with Mary, but that couldn't be further from the truth. It was one trial after another. Why is it important to be able to separate what God says about us from what he allows to happen in our lives?

_____

_____

_____

_____

_____

In Ephesians 1:6 the word *favor* means "freely accepted." Favor is simply the undeserved, unearned, unmerited *grace of God* giving us what we never could have earned ourselves—not even on our best day. What effect should the favor of God have on how we see ourselves, how we see the world we live in, and how we see our God?

_____

_____

_____

_____

_____

_____

In Luke 1:35 the angel said to Mary, *"The Holy Spirit will come upon you and the power of the Most High will overshadow you."* The person of the Holy Spirit is vital in every believer's life. How does the proclamation given to Mary play out in our lives?

_____

_____

_____

_____

_____

_____

_____

_____

_____

_____

THOUGHTS:

_____

_____

_____

_____

_____

_____

_____

_____

_____

_____

_____

_____

_____

_____

_____

_____

_____

_____

THOUGHTS:

CHAPTER 6: ABOVE ALL ELSE?

"Above all else, guard your heart, for everything you do flows from it" (Proverbs 4:23).

I'm a clean freak and as much as I love having a clean house there is something that is so much more important, we need clean hearts because our hearts are the Holy Spirit's home, and He deserves to live in a clean house. The only way to have a clean heart is by allowing the Word of God to wash us daily.

Oftentimes our standard of clean and God's standard of clean are very different. Sometimes the little things we learn to live with begin to dirty our hearts because they are totally unacceptable to God. But often we don't realize it until we come face-to-face with the light of God's Word. Psalm 119:130 states, *"The unfolding of your words give light; it gives understanding to the simple."* Once we have an encounter with the truth then what was acceptable before is no longer acceptable.

Maintaining a clean heart is a lifestyle and requires a brain wash! Solomon, the wisest of all men, could have chosen anything as the most important thing in life. But inspired by the Holy Spirit he penned Proverbs 4:23: *"Above all else, guard your heart for everything you do flows from it."*

"Above all else" means make this your number one priority; guard your own heart, for out of it flows all the issues of life. The Message puts it this way: *"Keep vigilant watch over your heart; that's where life starts."* In other words, Solomon is saying if you get it wrong here, you will get it wrong everywhere. Think about it this way: just as the earth spins on its axis, our hearts are the axis upon which everything in our lives spins. The heart is where all the action is!

Everything is filtered through the lens of the heart. It's the source of our perceptions and understanding. Therefore, it stands to reason that the heart calls the shots in our decision making process. As discussed earlier, the heart has the ability to think. Proverbs 23:7 states *"as a man thinks in is heart, so is he" (KJV).*

SATAN'S WEAPON OF CHOICE

Because the heart is such a vital part of our spiritual and emotional well-being, there's an enemy that wants a piece of the action. Satan wants to control the epicenter of our life to get it spinning out of control. His weapon of choice is *offense!* This *weapon of offense* has brought so many of God's people to a standstill. It's the number one cause of Christians falling away and going *AWOL*—all because their hearts were left unguarded and offense took root.

In Matthew 18:21-35, Peter asks Jesus how many times should we forgive a brother (sister) who offends us. The requirement under the Law states three times, so Peter went the extra mile and thought surely seven times was more than enough. Peter was not expecting Jesus' response, *"I tell you, not seven times, but seventy-seven times."*

The point wasn't the amount of times the lesson Jesus was trying to teach was that we must forgive that person as often as they need our forgiveness. Then Jesus goes on to tell a parable that clearly shows that we all owe a tremendous debt that we could never pay. That debt would have been attached to our family and all that we own. In the parable a merciful king who was owed a huge debt wanted to settle accounts, so he decided to wipe the slate clean and allow the debtor and his family to walk away scot free with all his possessions. The only requirement was the debtor would pay it forward. He would do unto others as it was done unto him.

The parable goes on to say that someone owed the forgiven debtor a much lesser amount, but this proud man didn't realize what had been done for him. This man represents all of us who often suffer from spiritual amnesia and hold on to offenses because we want the offender to pay for whatever wrong was done to us. We somehow feel we deserve forgiveness yet others don't deserve the same treatment. This kind of attitude is not acceptable to merciful Jesus. The outcome for the man that was forgiven his debt but wouldn't forgive the debt of another was that he was turned over to the jailers to be tortured, until he paid back all he owed.

The fact is, until we totally forgive we are bound up inside, tortured and imprisoned. In Matthew 18:35 Jesus states, *"This is how my heavenly Father will treat each of you unless you forgive your brother or sister from your heart."*

The only way to forgive is from the heart. When you forgive from your head and not from your heart, the old emotions that stem from your heart for being wronged keep washing away the thoughts in your mind that say you should forgive. Only when we act on God's Word can He begin to health our emotions and set us free from the captivity of offense.

BE QUICK TO MEND FENCES

The Bible says in Ephesians 4:3, *"Make every effort to keep the unity of the Spirit through the bond of peace."* Paul calls it an effort, which means it's not easy. He also states that the Holy Spirit brings the unity, but it's our responsibility to keep it. We keep it though the bond of peace, or as *The Message* puts it, we are to be *"quick to mend fences."* It's not only important to mend fences but we must do it quickly so we don't allow the devil to get a foot in.

Unity in the lives of believers was a major concern on the heart of Jesus because he knew that it would be a sign to the world (See: John 17:21). He wanted believers to be a unified front. Unity is tangible to the senses; where there is unity there is order and peace. Disunity is also tangible; and it is very off-putting. So can you see why the enemy wants to set us against one another? Can you see how we become nothing but pawns in the enemy's hands when we don't do things God's way? If we want to keep the enemy from succeeding in causing disunity, we must allow the Word of God and the Holy Spirit to have the run of the house!

LET'S PRAY

Lord, please allow my heart to be in line with Your Word. Please allow my heart to be humbled in Your presence, knowing that as You have forgiven me, I must quickly forgive others. Please keep my heart from being a place where the enemy is able to set up his base of operations. Rather, may my heart be a base of operations for the Holy Spirit to dismantle disunity in the body of Christ by my love and graciousness toward others. Teach me what it really means to forgive from the heart. I want my heart to be pleasing in your sight, dear Lord, in Jesus' name, Amen.

THOUGHTS FROM THE HEART:
In the following verses describe the condition of the heart:

Matthew 15:19

_____

_____

_____

Proverbs 12:25

_____

_____

_____

Jeremiah 17:9

_____

_____

_____

Psalm 14:1

_____

_____

_____

Psalm 34:18

_____

_____

_____

The Word of God washes us daily. Find three verses that describe the cleansing power of God's Word.

_____

_____

_____

_____

_____

_____

Satan's weapon of choice is offense. In the following three verses explain how we can combat the weapon of offense.

Proverbs 17:9

_____

_____

_____

Proverbs 10:12

_____

_____

_____

Proverbs 19:11

_____

_____

_____

SMALL GROUP DISCUSSION QUESTIONS:

Read the parable in Matthew 18:21-35. Describe a time in your own personal life when you had difficulty forgiving someone. Why was it so hard to forgive and how did holding on to the offense affect you both emotionally and spiritually.

_____

_____

_____

_____

Discuss the importance of unity in the Body of Christ and why do you think this was such a major concern on the heart of Jesus.

_____

_____

_____

_____

Why does the enemy want to set us up against one another? How does disunity affect our spiritual growth?

_____

_____

_____

_____

THOUGHTS:

_____

_____

_____

_____

_____

_____

_____

_____

_____

_____

_____

_____

_____

_____

_____

_____

_____

THOUGHTS:

CHAPTER 7: HEART ATTACKS

"Blessed is he who is not offended because of Me" (Luke 7:23, NKJV).

Offense happens to the best of us! When God isn't doing what we expect Him to do for us in our present circumstances, offense can easily slip right in, and we can start to question the sovereignty of God. I believe that's what happened to John the Baptist in Matthew 11:2-6. The Bible says when John was in prison, he heard about the things Jesus was doing, and he sent his disciples to ask Him, *"Are you the one who is to come, or should we expect someone else?"*

Even after all that John had seen with his own eyes and heard with his own ears, his present circumstance caused him to question the authenticity of Jesus.

How often have we been offended because of what God has allowed to happen to us or because of what He didn't allow to happen to us? Failed expectations and disappointments are a great source of offense.

Jesus goes to great lengths to prepare his disciples (and that includes us) of things that are bound to happen. Jesus said to his disciples that offenses will certainly come (See: Luke 17:1). This is a definite. Offense is inevitable. Be prepared for it to happen between brothers and sisters, and people close to you in the church community.

How we handle offense is the litmus test of our spiritual maturity. It seems in Luke 17:1 Jesus is saying that offense comes without warning, sort of like a heart attack. Yes, that's precisely what offense is—an attack on the heart! The word *offense* comes from the Greek work *skandalon*, which is where we get the word *scandal* or *scandalous*. It seems to suggest something mischievous, premeditated and deceptive. As it would happen, *skandalon* also describes a small, unassuming block of wood that keeps a trapdoor to a cage open. Bait, specific to the intended target, is placed inside the cage, which is tailored to lure the right victim. The target accidentally knocks into the *skandalon*, or the block of wood or "stumbling block," and suddenly the door slams shut, trapping the victim inside.[1]

So do you think it is safe to say that offense is a setup, a lure, a trap, a stumbling block that suddenly blindsides us, entrapping us in a cage of negative emotions? The enemy's goal is to cage us in bitterness and resentment. If we allow ourselves to be entrapped by offense, he will have us where he wants us.

When offense is not properly dealt with, the offended usually become the offender. That's why Jesus says in Luke 17:3, *"Watch yourselves.* He's really saying, *"Guard your heart. Don't worry about the offender, I'll take care of him."*

Keep your heart clean at all cost, if you think being hurt by someone you love is bad, just wait till you see what bitterness and resentment will do to you. Not only will offense destroy your peace, it will also totally change who you are. Offense is like having a leech inside your heart. It will suck out your anointing and purpose and drain all your strength and creativity. Offense contaminates your heart so that every word you speak and decision you make will be filtered through the lens of offense. Keep your heart clean, because your life choices are at stake.

DESTROYED BY OFFENSE

"A brother offended is harder to win than a strong city" (Proverbs 18:19a, NKJV).

Let's look throughout the Bible to see how holding on to an offense wrecked the call of God on so many people. These people had great potential to change their surroundings, but instead they caused great destruction, all because of offense.

Absalom: Accidentally was hung (See: 2 Samuel 13). He had the potential to be a great influencer, but he ended up causing great division and chaos in his father's kingdom.

Ahithophel: Hung himself (See: 2 Samuel 16). He was once the oracle of God, but became the mouthpiece of Satan.

Judas: Hung himself (See: John 12). He was once a trusted disciple, but became a betrayer.

Hanging onto offense is spiritual suicide!

THE SYCAMINE TREE

Going back to Luke 17:3-6 Jesus brings up the connection between forgiveness and faith. It takes an increase of faith to forgive when you have been offended. In verse 6 Jesus draws a parallel to the sycamine tree. In verse 1 Jesus starts his conversation talking about *skandalon,* thus likening offense to a small, unassuming block of wood, and ends with speaking about one of the largest, weightiest trees there was at the time. The example is: the small offense has become something massive!

The sycamine tree wasn't a random pick. It was known to have the most complicated root system. Rabbis believed it would take six hundred years to untangle the roots (which was the life expectancy of the tree). In addition, this tree was unusual because it grew and thrived best in dry conditions, it produced bitter figs, and its wood was used to make caskets. Jesus knew that when offense is not dealt with, it has the same potential as that tree:

- Offenses outlive us and can be handed down from generation to generation.
- Roots of offense entangle every area of our lives.
- Offenses are hard to kill.
- When we are offended, we thrive in dryness, we produce bitter fruit and we are surround by death.

It's best to deal with something small before it becomes something major. There's only one other massive, weighty tree that can counteract the massive, weighty tree of offense and that is Calvary's tree!

We have a choice today: forgive and let go or *hang on* and let it grow! When we forget what Jesus did for us by *hanging* on the cross, we *hang* onto the offense, and the rest of our lives will *hang* in the balance.

Jesus gives us the way out, he said to pray for your enemies and bless those who *"despitefully use you"* (Matthew 5:44 KJV). This is the real test of your spiritual maturity and character development. Dealing with the *weighty matters* of the heart is what grows us up and causes us to become mature giants in the faith!

LET'S PRAY

Dear Lord, I want to be all that You have called me to be, and I certainly don't want my anointing to be infected with the disease of offense-itis. I don't want to live in the land of offense, but I want to live in the land of the living. I want my feet to climb to higher heights as my heart is set free to soar. So I release the weights that have held my heart down one by one. Free Your servant, Lord. Let it be done unto me according to Thy Word, and may Your kingdom come down and explode in my heart on earth as it is in heaven. In Jesus' name, Amen!

THOUGHTS FROM THE HEART:

You previously were instructed to read the accounts of three lives that had great potential to change their surroundings but instead they caused great destruction, all because of offense. Describe what offended each person, and what was their outcome:

Absalom (Read 2 Samuel 13).

_____

_____

_____

Ahithophel (Read 2 Samuel 16).

_____

_____

_____

Judas (Read John 12).

_____

_____

_____

In Luke 17:1-5 Jesus instructs the disciples on what to do when you are offended. Describe in your own words what is necessary to overcome a personal offense.

_____

_____

_____

_____

_____

_____

Read Matthew 11:2-3. Describe in your own words why John the Baptist sent his disciples to ask Jesus, *"Are you the one who was to come or should we expect someone else?"*

_____

_____

_____

_____

_____

_____

_____

_____

List three Scriptures that warn against harboring offenses.

_____

_____

_____

_____

_____

_____

_____

_____

_____

SMALL GROUP DISCUSSION QUESTIONS:

Discuss with your group a time when you were personally *offended* and how that affected your spiritual walk.

_____

_____

_____

Now discuss a time when you were the *offender* and how that affected your spiritual walk.

_____

_____

_____

Has there ever been a time that you questioned the authenticity of Jesus as the Son of God? If so, what caused you to question and how did that play out in your life?

_____

_____

_____

_____

In Luke 17:5 the apostles asked Jesus to *"increase our faith."* In your own words how is our faith increased?

_____

_____

_____

_____

THOUGHTS:

_____

_____

_____

_____

_____

_____

_____

_____

_____

_____

_____

_____

_____

_____

_____

_____

_____

THOUGHTS:

CHAPTER 8: COMPLEXES . . . WILL THEY EVER GO AWAY?

"My grace is all you need. My power works best in weakness"
(2 Corinthians 12:9, NLT).

C omplexes are complex! They shape how we see ourselves. They overshadow nearly everything we do. We all have them I don't think there's a person on the planet that doesn't feel flawed in some way, shape or form. When we look in the mirror we all see our imperfections due to rejection, insensitive putdowns, failures or disappointments.

In 2 Corinthians 12 the apostle Paul speaks of weaknesses caused by a thorn in the flesh. One of the definitions of the word translated *weakness* in 2 Corinthian 12:9 is distressing, unsettling emotions. It would stand to reason that unsettling emotions could cause a person to feel fainthearted, weak or needy.

The apostle Paul admitted that he too had weaknesses, frailties and unsettling emotions caused by a thorn in the flesh sent by Satan to buffet him (v. 7). The Greek word translated *thorn* in verse 7 means something that causes severe pain or constant irritation. Some believe that it was a physical ailment, but I believe Paul was emotionally tormented. This thorn was sent by Satan to throw Paul off his game. But we know that anything the enemy throws at us, God will use for His benefit.

DRAWN TO THE SCARS

Strangely enough, our imperfections often are the very things that cause others to identify with us. Aren't we usually drawn to people who are willing to be real and show their weaknesses than to those who seem to be perfect? God is also attracted to imperfect people. In 1 Corinthians 1:27 the Bible says that God uses the foolish things to confound the wise.

There are numerous people that God has used that suffered from complexes that challenged the call of God on their lives. It has been said that D.L Moody had a complex because he was uneducated,[1] and the highly educated orator Charles Spurgeon suffered from deep, unsettling emotions.[2] In addition, there are several figures in the Bible who clearly must have wrestled with complexes.

LESSONS FROM DAVID

In 1 Samuel 16 the Lord sent Samuel the prophet to Jesse of Bethlehem because God had chosen one of his sons to be king. David, the youngest and least likely, was anointed in the presence of his father and brothers, and from that day on the Spirit of the Lord came upon David in power (1 Samuel 16:13). But in Chapter 17 Jesse sent David as a *delivery boy* to bring his brothers, who were with Saul in battle with the Philistines, some supplies, to see how they were doing and bring back some assurance from them (1 Samuel 17:17-19). When David walked onto the battlefield, Eliab mocked him, Saul laughed at him and Goliath scorned him. In the midst of that humiliation David did several things that I believe were significant to his future success, things that can teach us how to handle the curveballs life often throws at us:

- *David laid down his burden.* The bible says that as soon as David walked onto the battlefield he left the things he was carrying with the keeper of supplies (See: 1 Samuel 17:22). This tells me that we cannot be successful fighting the battle if we are weighed down with the things people put on us.
- *David ignored the taunts.* When David arrived at the battlefield his brother Eliab immediately attacked him (See: 1 Samuel 17:28). But David turned away and spoke about the matter with someone else (v. 30). When people try to discourage and accuse you, don't defend yourself, turn away and keep going forward. Always remember that God is your defender.
- *David stayed true to himself.* (See: 1 Samuel 17:33; 38-39) This tells me we all have our own armor we don't need to wear anyone else's we just need to be our self! Because the Spirit of the Lord had come upon David in power, he was able to stand against every scheme of the enemy. Thus he was used regardless of being the least likely candidate.

The Bible is filled with lives of men and women will complexes that God used to further His kingdom. There are so many life lessons that we can learn if we would just allow the Word of God to give us a brain wash!

GOD'S STRENGTH IN OUR WEAKNESS

The life of Moses (See: Exodus 2-4), is a great example to us that regardless of our background and our circumstances, complexes are really about how *we* see ourselves. Moses' life had many twists and turns that finally led him to the far side of the desert that ultimately became holy ground. The burning bush speaks and calls Moses' name and tells him God wants to use him. God is going to fulfill the deepest passion that Moses ever had, which was to see his fellow Israelites go free. But this time God is going to be the fuel behind his passion, not Moses' anger. God would use his weakness of speech to accomplish God's plan for His people. But Moses had a hard time grasping or comprehending that God wanted to make public his speech impediment. God wanted to put on display the very thing Moses wanted to hide. Isn't it incredible that we can have an encounter with God—we can see a bush on fire that speaks and just happens to know our name—but all that can pale in comparison to our complex, our thorn, our constant source of irritation and conflict, those insecurities that torment us.

Like Moses, the thorn—the complex stays, because it's in our weakness, in our distressing, unsettling emotions, that God's power is made perfect (See: 2 Corinthians 12:9)! This is God's assurance that we will keep relying on Him! We need to come to the realization that what God has called us to has little to do with us, and everything to do with Him. We have to stop despising our weaknesses, because they are really all we have to offer!

It's time to go the eighteen-inch distance and allow the brains of our hearts to be washed from all our twisted thinking that believes a perfect God wants only perfect vessels. Perfect vessels don't exist; only God is perfect. It's time to start believing that we are exactly what God wants to use, so that He alone can receive all the glory and honor.

LET'S PRAY

Dear Lord, please allow me to change the things that I boast about. Let me start to boast in my weaknesses and not my strengths, knowing that it's only in my weaknesses that Your strength is made perfect. Allow me to realize that You would never put me in any place or on any stage without totally covering me with Your anointing. I thank You for Your gracious mercy, and I thank You for every weakness that causes me daily to depend upon You. In Jesus' name, Amen!

THOUGHTS FROM THE HEART:

Read 2 Corinthians 12:1-10. in three different translations of the Bible. There are two types of boasting that Paul is comparing. Describe in your own words the comparison and what type of boasting is beneficial to our spiritual growth and character, and why is it beneficial.

_____

_____

_____

_____

_____

_____

Read 1 Samuel 17. Write out the character traits of David that are displayed when Eliab mocks him, Saul laughs at him and Goliath scorned him.

_____

_____

_____

_____

_____

Explain whom Eliab, Saul and Goliath represent in your own personal life.

Eliab:

_____

_____

Saul:

_____

_____

Goliath:

_____

_____

Read Exodus 2-4. In Exodus 3 what was Moses response when God informed him that he would be sent to Pharaoh to bring the Israelites out of Egypt?

_____

_____

_____

Why do you think Moses responded in that manner?

_____

_____

How did God respond to Moses?

_____

_____

How does this apply to your personal life?

_____

_____

<u>SMALL GROUP DISCUSSION QUESTIONS</u>:

Now that you're aware that we all struggle in life with complexes can you share with your group something that the Holy Spirit brought to light that might have hindered you from being effective in God's call on your life.

_____

_____

_____

With the examples that were given regarding the life of David and Moses do you see any comparisons or differences in how they handled their complexes?

_____

_____

_____

Are you transparent enough to show your weaknesses or do you strife to be perfect and make every effort to put up a front so people only see your strengths? How has that affected your relationship with God and others?

_____

_____

_____

Find two other people in the bible that had complexes and describe how those unsettling emotions affected their calling.

_____

_____

_____

THOUGHTS:

_____

_____

_____

_____

_____

_____

_____

_____

_____

_____

_____

_____

_____

_____

_____

_____

_____

THOUGHTS:

_____

_____

_____

_____

_____

_____

_____

_____

_____

_____

_____

_____

_____

_____

_____

_____

CHAPTER 9: THERE IS TREASURE IN THE TRASH

"I know that through your prayers and God's provision of the Spirit of Jesus Christ what has happened to me will turn out for my deliverance " (Philippians 1:19).

Have you ever wondered if the Lord could ever use your situation or mess? I think too often, because we cannot imagine how good could possibly come out of bad, we allow our pain to be wasted. But be assured that our trials and struggles are *recyclable!* To recycle is to convert waste into reusable material, because there are substances in the waste that are redeemable and still have value.

God is in the recycling business. Long before there were environmentalists, God knew He could create something redeemable out of what seems like life's wasteful moments. The all-seeing God knows that there is treasure in our trash!

There is so much potential in our pain even though we can't immediately see its future value in its present state. Would you believe that some of the backpacks that children carry to school were once dirty old plastic beverage bottles? The new item has absolutely no resemblance to the original. In a similar way everything we've gone through or will go through can be used for someone else's benefit. Everything in our life can be repurposed to bring comfort and healing to someone else.

MORE THAN MEETS THE EYE

We don't realize that our pain has the potential to be somebody else's eternal gain, that our mess has the potential to become a message of hope to the hopeless. Everything we have been through has the potential to become a life lesson for someone else. The apostle Paul said that *"everything"* that happened to him was to advance the gospel (Philippians 1:12; 18-22). Paul said, *"They didn't shut me up, they gave me a pulpit" (Philippians 1:18, MSG).*

The Bible puts everybody's *stuff* out there because the anointing to minister is really in yesterday's sweat and struggle. The blessing is not only in the pain we have endured, but it's also in the pain we may have caused. It's easier to share our pain from a victim's standpoint. But sharing our own failures and the sin we have repented of on this long journey of sanctification, is equally important and beneficial to our growth process and the growth in others. I always say, *"Let your trials pay you dividends—double for the trouble—and bring others much-needed relief."*

But in order for that to happen, we must be set free from associating our failures with shame. People are more ministered to by our weaknesses than by our perfections. Our scars tell the story that people need to hear!

GOD USES EVERYTHING

Jesus told Peter, *"Satan has asked to sift you as wheat. But I have prayed for you, Simon that your faith may not fail. And when you have turned back, strengthen your brothers"* (Luke 22:31-32). What Jesus was actually saying is:

> *"You are going to have a blip in your faith. But don't worry I'm praying that you won't give up the fight! And when you return, don't hide it. Push past the pain and the shame. Use your failure to encourage others. Allow the Holy Spirit to extract from your horrible experience something substantial to help someone else."*

Look at Paul's frustration with failure and defeat. In Romans 7 he says the very things he wants to do he doesn't, and the things he doesn't want to do, he ends up doing. In verse 24 he says, *"Oh wretched and weary man that I am! Who can save me from this body that is subject to death?"*

But because he confesses his mess, God squeezes out a message! In Romans 8:1 he writes, *"Therefore, there is now no condemnation for those who are in Christ Jesus."*

Paul's pain now becomes our gain. His struggle has been recycled to bring hope to our struggling lives!

God even uses heinous sins. You can see this in the life of David when he sinned with Bathsheba and then had her husband killed so he could hide his sin. Few people knew what David had done, but God sent the prophet Nathan to expose David's sin (See: 2 Samuel 12). David could have made excuses but he didn't. And once David confessed his sin, God released an anointing that would minister to others. That's the key to revival! Out of David's mess we get the message of Psalm 32.

In the Book of Ruth, you read how God turned Naomi's bitterness into an anointing that gave hope to her daughter-in-law and ultimately every person that reads her story. The story starts off with a famine, but it ends with a crop of righteousness that is still produced to this day!

Charles Spurgeon said:

"Why do we dread the clouds that darken our sky? It is true that for a while the dark clouds hide the sun, but it is not extinguished and it will soon shine again. Meanwhile those clouds are filled with rain, and the darker they are, the more likely they are to bring plentiful showers."[1]

It has been said the A.W. Tozer often felt like a miserable failure, and Andrew Bonar said he often felt deep regret. In each story we can see how the Lord redirected, repurposed, recycled and transformed so many different kinds of people and circumstances. There is nothing that the Master cannot redeem for His glory!

We too have quite a story to tell once we have the courage to be honest and share it. We are salve for the weary, balm for the broken, dressing for the burned, and medicine for this sin-sick world. So let's allow the Holy Spirit to lift our burden and break the yoke so what's valuable can be extracted. We're only eighteen inches from a victory if we would only allow the Holy Spirit to use our past.

"As for you, you've been given an anointing, which you received from Him, and it resides permanently in you" (1 John 2:27).

LET'S PRAY

Precious Holy Spirit, please open my eyes to see that my past trash can become someone else's treasure today as I share with them in total honesty what You can do with a life no matter how stinky it is at the present time. Give me the courage to share the good, the bad, and the ugly, and allow me to tell others how You recycled all me fears, insecurities, and failures. Lord, allow Your work of grace to continue through my testimony, in Jesus' name, Amen!

THOUGHTS FROM THE HEART:

Read Philippians 1:12-30. Describe how Paul's chains advanced the gospel.

_____

_____

_____

What was the most important thing to Paul?

_____

_____

_____

Read Luke 22. Jesus addressed Simon Peter as the leader and spokesman of the apostles. The plural _you_ indicates Satan wanted to sift _all_ the apostles like wheat, a rough action that symbolizes tempting them to spiritual ruin. What does that imply to you personally?

_____

_____

_____

What was the initial outcome of Satan's sifting? How does that apply to your life?

_____

_____

_____

How can we overcome Satan's sifting?

_____

_____

_____

SMALL GROUP DISCUSSION QUESTIONS:

Discuss with the group ways that we can each personally advance the gospel.

_____

_____

_____

Read 2 Samuel 12:14. Describe how David initially responded to the prophet Nathan. Once David realized that Nathan was talking about him how did he change his response? How do you respond when confronted with a sin you have committed?

_____

_____

_____

_____

_____

_____

Discuss with the group how a mistake you made in your personal life was used to bring hope to someone else.

_____

_____

_____

_____

_____

_____

THOUGHTS:

THOUGHTS:

_____

_____

_____

_____

_____

_____

_____

_____

_____

_____

_____

_____

_____

_____

_____

_____

_____

THOUGHTS:

CHAPTER 10: ALL ACCESS

"Let us then approach God's throne of grace with confidence, so that we may receive mercy and find grace to help us in our time of need" (Hebrews 4:16).

T he Bible tells us that as new covenant believers we have all access to the Father. Ephesians 2:18 states, *"For through him we both have access to the Father by one Spirit."* We *all* have reserved seats in heaven's most sacred place. The term *new covenant* simply means *new arrangement*. A new arrangement has been made to get us into a place we would never have been allowed to go.

In the Old Testament the common man was absolutely *not* allowed to enter the holy places of the tabernacle. The high priest alone went behind the veil. The veil was a thick curtain—a massive, imposing wall of separation sixty feet high and thirty feet wide. Jewish historians say it took three hundred priests to move it.

All access: no limits, no restrictions.
Access: the act of bringing to, a moving to; approach.[1]

NO LIMITS

The message God obviously wanted to send was there were places in the tabernacle that were *off limits*. Even the high priest had restrictions. He only had access one time per year on the Day of Atonement. If the high priest wasn't right before God, he would fall dead behind that massive curtain, and someone would have to use a long staff to pull him out. So as much as being a high priest was a privilege, the position probably brought with it a lot of fear, dread, anxiety, and even panic. There was torment attached to the position, because if the priest made a mistake, he could end up dead!

But all that changed in the New Testament, in Matthew 27:51 the Bible declares that when Jesus gave up His Spirit, simultaneously miles away in the temple, that massive veil, the imposing wall of separation was torn from top to bottom. Now *whoever believes* can go inside (John 3:16). There is now an open door giving us all access for communication between God and us. Under the new arrangement both the minister and layperson *all* have access *all the time* to come into the presence of God with *boldness* (Hebrews 4:16). That's the posture God wants us to have when we enter into His presence.

Boldness: free and fearless confidence, cheerful courage, and assurance.[2]

The basis of our boldness is the blood of Jesus.

"Therefore, brothers and sisters, since we have confidence to enter the Most Holy Place by the blood of Jesus...let us draw near to God with a sincere heart and with the full assurance that faith brings, having our hearts sprinkled to cleanse us from a guilty conscience and having our bodies washed with pure water" (Hebrews 10:19, 22).

The only reason you and I are allowed to draw near to God with boldness is the blood of Jesus. Leviticus 17:11 states, *"For the life of a creature is in the blood, and I have given it to you to make atonement for yourselves on the altar; it is the blood that makes atonement for ones life."*

The spiritual life of the believer is faith in the precious blood of Jesus! It's nothing but the blood that washes away our sin, and that makes us whole again. It cleanses us; it redeems us; it justifies us; and it qualifies us! If we should by chance slip, fall, or stumble into sin, God looks at the spotless Lamb as our substitute, because our life is hidden in Christ.

CONFIDENCE: FIRM AND UNSHAKEABLE

Because of the blood of Jesus we have confidence. The word *confidence* is used thirty-one times in the New Testament. The word means firm and unshakable. It indicates a sense of complete freedom—freedom that comes from an intimate relationship with God and full assurance of our acceptance by Him. Hebrews 10:20 states that the curtain opened a new and living way. This way is refreshing and life giving, not filled with dread, condemnation, or death!

To accept this there has to be a paradigm shift in the very core of our being; otherwise, we will live as the Old Testament priests did—under the law of fear and dread each time we approach the throne. That is why the Bible warns us in Hebrews 10:35, *"Do not throw away your confidence."*

It also states in 1 John 3:21 (NKJV), *"Beloved, if our heart does not condemn us, we have confidence toward God."*

SIN: MEANS TO MISS THE MARK

When we sin, *just confess it; don't dress it!* Sin doesn't cause us to lose our position with God, but it does block our fellowship with Him. The word *confess* doesn't mean to beg, plead, or live in misery. It simply means to agree with God concerning our sin. It's like the parable of the prodigal son; he never stopped being a son, but because he went far away, he lost fellowship, communication, and even his privileges as a son (See: Luke 15:11-32). But he didn't consider himself a son any longer, but was willing to go back and be one of the hired hands. The way he saw himself was so the opposite of the way his father saw him. When he returned the only thing his father cared about was that his son was now home, there were no limits, no boundaries to the amount of grace that father had to give his son.

The more we understand the magnificent, amazing grace of God, the quicker, the greater, and the more magnanimous our confession will be. We won't wrap our confession in blame, we will simply be ever so grateful that the One who knows us the best wants to quickly relieve us of anything that would cause a breach in our relationship.

WHY THE CONFLICT?

So why is there such an internal conflict? What is the enemy of our confidence? *The enemy of our confidence is our conscience!* Our conscience is in conflict with our confidence. Our conscience is our innermost soul and consciousness. It's our moral barometer. It's where we get our moral sensitivity or scruples. This was put in us by God to show us right from wrong, and it works in conjunction with the law. The problem with our conscience is that the very thing that convicts us accuses us.

Our conscience is our prosecutor, whereas our confidence is our advocate. Our conscience keeps us conscious of *all* our flaws, weaknesses and faults. It tells us we don't deserve to approach God with boldness! Confidence, on the other hand, keeps me conscious of all that Jesus is and all He has done on my behalf.

Hebrews 9:9 states that all the gifts and sacrifices offered under the old covenant weren't enough to clear the conscience of the worshipper. Notice the Bible declares it was the conscience of the worshippers that needed to be cleared. This is why God scrapped the old system and made a new arrangement. The problem with the old covenant was that the worshipper was unable to feel clean! Hebrews 10:2-3 states that the repeated sacrifices were just a reminder of the people's sins.

But here's the good news: *"How much more, then, will the blood of Christ…cleanse our consciences from acts that lead to death, so that we may serve the living God" (Hebrews 9:14)?*

When Jesus was on the cross He said, *"It is finished"* (John 19:30); then he later sat down at the right hand of the Father (Mark 16:19); and now intercedes for you and me (Romans 8:34).

The debt we once owed could never be paid back, and God doesn't expect us to repay it. The only outstanding debt that we now owe is to love one another (Romans 13:8). We are just to pay God's love forward! We must live to give out the same mercy to others that we've been given. We are to love with the same measure with which we have been loved, that is what pleases the heart of God.

The apostle Paul tells Timothy, his son in the faith, *"The only way you can fight the good fight of faith is by holding on to faith and a good conscience"* (1 Timothy 1:18-19, *my paraphrase*).

The dynamic duo:
- *Faith:* in the finished work of Jesus Christ, not faith in faith or faith in good works.
- *Good Conscience:* the knowledge that you are in right standing with God because of the blood of Jesus.

The revelation of God's Word brings about a revolution. This is revolutionary thinking that must transpire in our inner most being—eighteen inches from our head to our heart!

LETS PRAY

Father, I want to thank you for sending Jesus in my place. Thank You, Jesus, for shedding Your precious blood for all sins—the one's I committed and the ones I will commit. I will not trample underfoot the Son of God or insult the Spirit of Grace by knowingly and callously sinning. Nor will I insult You any longer by not accepting the finished work of the cross, because I now understand that when you said, "It is finished," You meant exactly that. I will never try to add anything else to what You have done except to pay forward the mercy You have freely given me by Your grace. In Jesus' name, Amen!

THOUGHTS FROM THE HEART:

Describe in your own words why God wants us to approach Him with boldness.

_____

_____

_____

List three significant differences between the Old and New Testaments when is comes to our right standing and relationship with the Father.

_____

_____

_____

Read Luke 15:11-32. After the Prodigal Son squandered all his wealth there was a famine in the land and he began to be in need. Now he came to realization of all that he lost and wanted to return back to his father's house. How did he plan on returning? What did his plan reveal about his relationship with his father.

_____

_____

_____

_____

_____

_____

_____

_____

SMALL GROUP DISCUSSION QUESTIONS:

Our conscience is our prosecutor, whereas our confidence is our advocate. Discuss how this plays out in the life of a born again believer?

_____

_____

_____

_____

_____

_____

Why is the new covenant so liberating? How should we be living our lives as new covenant believers?

_____

_____

_____

_____

_____

_____

Read 1 Timothy 1:15-17. Paul states twice in these verses, _"I was shown mercy,"_ and then goes on to explain the result of that mercy in his life. Discuss with your group the effect that God's mercy has had on your life.

_____

_____

_____

_____

_____

THOUGHTS:

_____

_____

_____

_____

_____

_____

_____

_____

_____

_____

_____

_____

_____

_____

_____

_____

_____

THOUGHTS:

CHAPTER 11: GETTING TO THE ROOT OF DEPRESSION

"Anxiety in the heart of man causes depression" (Proverbs 12:25a, NKJV).

When we think of depression, we naturally think of an illness of the mind, which is definitely true in the medical sense. There are definite chemical imbalances in the brain that can cause extreme mood swings. But clearly the verse in Proverbs 12:25 is not addressing depression caused by a chemical or hormonal condition. I believe it is speaking about being overwhelmed by life's circumstances and curveballs that come our way and cause *spiritual depression.*

God's Word is full of people who suffered from this malady in one way, shape or form, and unfortunately it is still affecting many of God's people today. Believers and non-believers alike are convinced in their hearts and minds that God has abandoned them. They fear that either God doesn't see their situation, or that He just doesn't care. When it comes to fear, worry and anxiety both the head and the heart are involved. The worries of life that start in our head find a home in our heart.

The apostle Paul in Philippians 4:6-7 strongly exhorts:

"Do not be anxious about anything, but in every situation, by prayer and petition, with thanksgiving, present your requests to God. And the peace of God, which transcends all understanding, will guard your hearts and your minds in Christ Jesus."

Clearly we see that nursing anxious thoughts infiltrates both the head and the heart. Paul prays for God to guard them both, because once anxiety is allowed to take root, depression is sure to follow.

Proverbs 12:25 seems to zero in on to the heart as the base where anxiety seems to rest it's ugly head and then spreads out and weaves itself into the fabric of our daily lives. David said, *"From the ends of the earth I call to you. I call as my heart grows faint; lead me to the rock that is higher than I" (Psalm 61:2).*

David knew that it would take far more than positive thinking to unravel the darkness that was pulling him into the oblivion of spiritual depression. It would take the divine hand of God to pull him up from the gravitational pull that would try to take him down. Only the light of God could pierce the darkness and give him faith to go on.

From the moment Samuel anointed David as the next king, David's heart had many opportunities to be weighed down with negative data: David was just the *nobody* of his dysfunctional family who was left to guard the flocks; he was ridiculed by his brother; he was looked down upon by King Saul because he didn't have the proper armor; and mocked by Goliath because his weapon was meager, to say the least. Chased by King Saul, a jealous madman for ten years. And the list goes on and on. Take some time to read through 1 and 2 Samuel to get the full picture of all that David went through that caused him to experience *the dark night of the soul.*

HOPE IN GOD!

Depression in the heart! What anguish David must have lived through yet he kept looking to the Lord, commanding his soul to *"hope in God!"* We clearly see throughout the Psalms that this was the strategy that David used in dealing with overwhelming thoughts of despair. In some of his psalms he would begin by recounting his sorrows and remembering his enemies, and then end it by recalling the goodness of God. David writes:

> *"Though an army besiege me, my heart will not fear, though war break out against me, even then I will be confident. I remain confident of this: I will see the goodness of the Lord in the land of the living" (Psalm 27:3, 13).*

Another great psalmist was Asaph who also went through a terrible bout with spiritual depression (See: Psalm 73). The enemy tried to take him out and tried to take away his song. But he fixed his eyes on the Lord and continued to lead the people in anointed worship, which is what he was created to do!

The only thing that can save us from the snare of negative thinking is the power of God's Word. It's a weapon onto itself. Every written word on the page becomes alive as we receive it inside our hearts. It then becomes our fuel and rips to shreds the thoughts that want to weigh us down and rob our peace (See: Hebrews 4:12).

Let's look at the life of Elijah (1 Kings Chapter 17 – 2 Kings Chapter 2), the most powerful prophet ever to have lived. He was a man full of God's power but he too experienced great highs and great lows, just as we do. In James 5:17, the Bible states, *"Elijah was a human being, even as we are."*

One great attribute of Elijah was that he lived by the command of God, and without doubt or complaint he went where God directed him to go. Elijah was led to the most unlikely places and at every juncture his faith was tested. And just like us Elijah would battle with disappointment, discouragement and despondency. He often went from faith to fear in a New York minute. He actually got to the point of wanting God to take his life (See: 1 Kings 19:4). This was one exhausted, battle-weary man of God. What could possibly have happened? I believe after all was said and done it appeared to him that nothing had really changed in his conquest with Ahab and Jezebel. He just lost hope!

HEARTSICK

After three and a half years of sacrifice and dedication, Elijah was spiritually depressed. His heart took a nosedive into the depths of despair. Disappointment precedes depression. It's amazing that God can feed us by a raven and multiply flour and oil, but He won't change someone's heart that refuses to yield to the writing on the wall. The Bible states in Proverbs 13:12a that: *"Hope deferred makes the heart sick."*

How many of us have been heartsick? How many of us have been spiritually depressed and didn't want to admit that we were going through the "dark night of the soul?"

So Elijah, the human being, *"even as we are,"* retreated from the desert into the cave of self-pity. Satan loves when we go into the cave of self-pity. He loves when we isolate ourselves and never ask others to help us pray. Thank God the angel showed up and spoke to Elijah's heart and straightened him out (See: 1 Kings 19:13)! *"What are you doing here, Elijah?"*

How many times has the Lord sent us an angel to speak a Word of faith into our heart to revive and refresh us? Our hearts must be refreshed by the Word of God daily so the toxins of yesterday find no root in our hearts today.

There's always a way out of the valley, out of the desert, out of the cave! Jesus said in John 16:33b, *"In this world you will have trouble. But take heart! I have overcome the world."* Jesus could have said, *"Don't lose your mind,"* but He said, *"Don't lose heart."* Don't allow overwhelming thoughts that cause anxiety to settle in your heart and cause you to spiral down into spiritual depression.

We have no other choice than to heed the command the angel gave to Elijah in 1 Kings 19:5, *"Get up and eat."* Elijah responded but he laid back down again, so the angel came back a second time and touched him and said again, *"Get up and eat, for the journey is too much for you"* (vv.7).

This time Elijah ate, and he was sustained for a forty-day journey to Mount Horeb, the mountain of God. That is where God spoke to him in a still small voice (vv. 11-13). When we are going through a spiritual depression, we have to get to God and hear his still small voice that chases away the darkness inside. Elijah was instructed to go back the way he came!

Think about how we could glean from those instructions when we are in a spiritual depression. *"Go back the way you came."* In other words, change direction, make an about face, and go forward in the right direction. The Lord also told Elijah to anoint others—*empower others!* That's what all this testing has been about—to empower others! That our life would testify of the all-sufficient grace of God even when it *seems* all hope is gone!

Elijah was a human just like us. He had the same weaknesses, faced the same enemies as we do, and got discouraged. But we must also remember that we have the same resources and power that Elijah had. We have the

Holy Spirit, the Word of God and the body of Christ to help us fight our battles.

The one mistake Elijah made was thinking he was alone, and feeling like he was the only one going through a hard time. We need not make the same mistake by isolating ourselves. Remember you are not alone, nor are you the only one going through hard times. We would be far better off if we tapped into the resources that are within our reach. We should lock arms and form prayer groups until the spirit of Jezebel is thrown down from her high place! It's wartime, not peacetime!

LETS PRAY

Lord, heal me from this spiritual depression that has taken root inside my heart. Teach me how to train my inner man to look upward instead of looking inward. Teach me to fix my eyes on You. Give me the courage not to make peace with my situation. When my heart is overwhelmed with the troubles of life, lead me to the Rock, Christ Jesus. Don't allow me to settle for anything less than Your best for my life. I'm asking that you give me the strategy to take down every high place that mocks Your name so I can have Your peace that guards my heart and mind. And finally, Lord, give me a cheerful heart, which is good medicine—for any lingering spiritual depression. In Jesus' name, Amen!

THOUGHTS FROM THE HEART:

Take some time to read 1 Samuel 17 through 2 Samuel 2 and list at least six events in David's life that could have brought on a spiritual depression.

_____

_____

_____

David was a very disciplined young man, he did what the Bible tells us to do in 2 Corinthians 10:3-5. What are the weapons that are available to us to demolish the stronghold of spiritual depression?

_____

_____

_____

Read 2 Corinthians 4:16-18 and put into your own words the strategy that Paul is giving to believers to prevent spiritual depression from taking root in our hearts. (Read this Scripture portion in _at least three_ different translations to get a more accurate description of the strategy.)

_____

_____

_____

Read 1 Kings 19:1-9 and list what Elijah was feeling that caused him to get to the point of saying, _"I have had enough, Lord. Take my life."_

_____

_____

_____

SMALL GROUP DISCUSSION QUESTIONS:

James 5:17a states, *"Elijah was a human being, even as we are."* What does that imply regarding the struggles that we face in our daily lives?

_____

_____

_____

_____

_____

_____

David, Elijah and Paul are three examples in the Bible of people that had challenging circumstance in their lives that caused them to experience a temporary spiritual depression. What have you learn from their lives that can help with your own struggles with disappointment, discouragement, and depression?

_____

_____

_____

_____

_____

How can we encourage others that might be struggling with spiritual depression?

_____

_____

_____

THOUGHTS:

THOUGHTS:

CHAPTER 12: STAND UP!

"Consider him who endured such opposition from sinners, so that you will not grow weary and lose heart" (Hebrews 12:3).

Every message we have ever heard came out of a royal mess! Yes, there are a lot of *gory* details before the *glory!* If we don't recognize this vital truth we will wonder why *our* problems aren't solved with instant answers and we will live in defeat and be named amongst the quitters.

The most challenging word to hear when your experiencing a trial of any proportion is *wait!* Unfortunately, too many people do not realize that there is such a thing as an appointed time because we live in the day of instant gratification. Our culture has set us up for the immediate and we are no longer wired for *the wait.*

"For the revelation awaits an appointed time; it speaks of the end, and will not prove false. Though it linger, wait for it, it will certainly come, and will not delay " (Habakkuk 2:3).

God has an appointed time to bring about the miracle you have been hoping for in your situation!

BARREN AND BROKEN

In 1 Samuel 1 we read about a woman who knew a lot about waiting, her name was Hannah. Her husband, Elkanah, had two wives the first was Hannah and the second was Peninnah. The Bible says that Hannah was barren but Peninnah had children and she would taunt Hannah, never letting her forget that God had not given her children. This went on *year after year* (See: 1 Samuel 1:1, 6-7).

Looking at Scripture, it is plain to see that there are some things in life that are chronic and out of our control. Hannah was a woman who loved God, and God loved her, yet she was not exempt from heartache and a long season of discouraging drought. She had no idea that God had an appointed time for her to conceive and like most of us, she probably couldn't see beyond her pain and grief.

The Bible is full of life stories of men and women who were devout believers that went through things that were chronic and out of their control. If we fail to understand that difficult things happen to good people we will end up spiritually paralyzed and emotionally discouraged. Jesus said,

"I have told you these things, so that in me you may have peace. In this world you will have trouble. But take heart! I have overcome the world" (John 16:33).

Because Hannah was barren, her husband Elkanah took another wife to carry on the family name. Elkanah was a Levite from a priestly line called the Kohathites. Under the Jewish law he was permitted to take on another wife to produce offspring to continue the priestly line. Hannah must have felt like a failure on multiple fronts, since God had closed her womb she was a disappointment physically and spiritually because she deprived her husband of carrying on his godly seed. And Peninnah took every opportunity to reinforce Hannah's negative feelings (See: 1 Samuel 1:6-7).

Bible commentators believe Peninnah had at least four sons and two daughters. To the natural eye she was blessed and loved by God, and Hannah was not. People usually judge whether a person is blessed by what they have obtained in life. This is just another indication that the brains of our hearts need to be washed. Outward circumstances are no indication of God's love and blessing. That's why it's so important that we have a personal revelation of the promises and character of God.

The Bible states that every year Elkanah took his family up to the sanctuary of God. And *every year* Hannah was taunted by Peninnah and would be so heartsick that even though she would get to God's house she would never get to God. Year after year she would leave the same way she came, never asking for what she needed from the only *one* who could grant her petition.

But 1 Samuel 1:9 says, that one day Hannah *"stood up"*! One day, after all those years, Hannah took a stand and said, *"Enough is enough!"* On that day faith replaced discouragement and her posture changed. She decided, *"I don't have to sit at the table of grief and despair when I could be standing in the presence of the Lord."*

She must have thought if God opened the wombs of Sarah and Rachel, then He could do it for her! She made contact with heaven and experienced a holy explosion. She stopped crying over what she didn't have and started to cry out for what she could have. Out of her anguish and grief she released a cry that got heaven's attention (See: 1 Samuel 1:8-20).

We now see a woman who was changed in the presence of the Lord, she was no longer in anguish and grief, but now has a new boldness and sense of expectancy. In the course of time Hannah conceived and gave birth to a son, and named him Samuel, saying, *"Because I asked the Lord for him."*

It was well worth the wait! Hannah not only received a son, but Israel received a man of God that would eventually change the nation. Thus the appointed time, when the gory details turned into glory!

THE GIFT OF FAITH

The one and only thing that works with God is for His holy nostrils to *smell faith!* Sometimes we go to church but we don't go to war! Sometimes we are so busy crying that we have forgotten how to cry out! Like Hannah we need to *stand up* and stop sitting at the table of anguish and grief. It's that *stand of faith* that gives a life-changing revelation that rewires the way the brain in our heart thinks. Faith is not a fruit of the Spirit, but it is a gift from God. It doesn't have to be cultivated you just have to ask God for the weapon of faith to tear down the chronic issue that has you spiritually paralyzed and emotionally discouraged. It's the gift of faith that gives boldness and expectancy to receive what you pray for, just like Hannah experienced that day when she finally took a stand and asked God for the desire of her *new* heart!

DON'T GIVE UP!

God needs to raise-up a church of Hannahs who will *stand up* and not *give up*, a church that will change its posture and refuse to accept lifelessness and barrenness. Now is the time to change your position, stand up and freely accept every blessing God has for you. You will know beyond the shadow of a doubt that you have made the eighteen-inch journey successfully when you start to immerse yourself daily in the pool of His amazing grace, accepting His love instead of rejecting it. As you receive His unconditional love it will empower you to love others, even the Peninnahs in your life. The revelation of His love will bring about a *revolution!*

Church we need a revolution and it must start with us! It starts in the fertile womb of a clean heart, which will be impregnated with the seed of the Holy Spirit so that we can give birth to spiritual children! Don't ever give up *stand up* and fight for what belongs to you. God's kingdom suffers violence, but the violent (in the spirit) take it by force (See: Matthew 11:12). There's always some *gory details* before He pours out His *glory*, but remember there is *an appointed time, wait for it, though it tarry, it will not delay!*

LET'S PRAY!

Lord, I don't have the gift of faith, but I am coming to You, the giver of the gift. I'm asking you to baptize me with the faith I need to believe that what You did for others, You will do for me. Give me the stamina to fight and wait until I see my prayers come to pass—until I see the "appointed time" come in my life. In Jesus' precious name, Amen!

THOUGHTS FROM THE HEART:

Read 1 Samuel Chapters 1 and 2, write out three character traits that you see in Hannah that indicates she was a God fearing woman.

_____

_____

_____

In 1 Samuel 1:15-17 Hannah explains to Eli her state of mind and heart. She describes herself as deeply troubled, with feelings of anguish and grief. Another word for grief in this verse is _resentment_. What was the source of Hannah's anguish and resentment?

_____

_____

_____

What caused Hannah to have a change of heart over her present condition?

_____

_____

_____

What type of prayer did Hannah pray to the Lord and how did the Lord respond to her prayer?

_____

_____

_____

_____

_____

SMALL GROUP DISCUSSION QUESTIONS:

Read Habakkuk 2:3. Discuss a time in your personal life when you prayed for a desire in your heart and the answer was delayed. How did that affect you spiritually and emotionally?

_____

_____

_____

Read Psalm 40 with your group. David starts out this psalm by saying, *"I waited patiently for the Lord; he turned to me and heard my cry."* Why is it important to wait patiently? How can we be patient while waiting for an answer from the Lord?

_____

_____

_____

_____

_____

Why do you think *waiting* on the Lord is so important to our spiritual maturity and growth?

_____

_____

_____

_____

_____

THOUGHTS:

_____

_____

_____

_____

_____

_____

_____

_____

_____

_____

_____

_____

_____

_____

_____

_____

THOUGHTS:

_____

_____

_____

_____

_____

_____

_____

_____

_____

_____

_____

_____

_____

_____

_____

_____

_____

_____

THOUGHTS:

_____

_____

_____

_____

_____

_____

_____

_____

_____

_____

_____

_____

_____

_____

_____

_____

_____

CONCLUSION: THE HEART OF THE MATTER

"Love the Lord your God with all your heart and with all your soul and with all your mind. This is the first and greatest commandment. And the second is like it: 'Love your neighbor as yourself'" (Matthew 22:37-39).

Throughout this book we have seen that the *heart* has a mind of its own, and that many of us need to rewire the way the brain of the heart thinks. The eighteen-inch journey from our mind to our heart is the pathway to victory.

In the passage of Matthew 22:37-39 Jesus makes no distinction between loving Him and loving our neighbor. He is saying that if we love Him without reservation, we will also love others in the same manner. The one and only way we could show God that we love Him is by loving our neighbor.

As born again believers we must allow God's love to travel down into the deepest recesses of our hearts so they can be melted and become like the very heart of God. When we don't allow the love of God to penetrate and permeate the hidden places of the heart and bring healing to it, we will be judgmental and prideful. We become people who, though *born again*, strain out a gnat but swallow a camel (See: Matthew 23:24).

Now here is the problem: It is impossible to love your neighbor as much as you love yourself if you don't love God with your *whole heart*. And it is impossible to love God with your *whole heart* unless your heart is whole! Do you now see why having a healthy heart is of the utmost importance?

A NEW LEVEL

Another major problem created when the heart is not whole is that we can't love ourselves, which we must do if we are to love one another. When we hate ourselves, we hate the world around us. So a vital part of loving with our whole heart is the ability to love our self. You see we first must receive God's love for us in order to love others. This is the law of love, *"heaven's law"* that promotes kindness and can only come from a heart that has been made whole.

The New Testament gives us another challenge. It tells us to not only love our neighbor as we love ourselves, but to also love our neighbor as Christ loved us! But we cannot accomplish this on our own we need the Holy Spirit to empower us to go to a *new level* of maturity and courage. To be able to love others as He has loved us takes real maturity and it's the apex of our faith.

God's Word challenges us in Hebrews 3:13-15 to encourage one another daily, as long as it's called *"today,"* lest the devil brings discouragement to our brothers and sisters, causing them to *lose heart*. In order to be an encourager, you need to be looking away from yourself to the betterment of others.

Did you know that in psychology there is something called *"withholding?"* The person whose heart is not whole will purposely withhold encouragement from someone else for fear that the encouraging word will put them on their same level. Unfortunately, this goes on in the body of Christ all the time. Oh, may the Holy Spirit make our whole heart healthy and practicing the gift of encouragement daily. *"Most importantly, love each other daily"* (1 Peter 4:8, NCV).

The law of love overlooks the flaws of others and extends love for the purpose of healing. We need to give mercy out the same way God poured His mercy into our lives, but if our hearts are not made whole, we will be blind to all the mercy that has been afforded to us.

The Bibles states in Romans 13:8, "Let no debt remain outstanding except the continuing debt to love one another." This is called paying it forward! My prayer is that the Holy Spirit will use this book and bible study to uproot the thorns that have been sown and cultivated in the ground of our hearts. Let's allow the Lord to replant seeds of His magnanimous love in our hearts so the world can taste and see that He is good!

LET'S PRAY!
Lord, please clean my heart thoroughly. Take Your scalpel and gut out all the infection that keeps my heart sick once and for all. Make me totally whole so I can finally fulfill the purpose I was created for. Allow me to be a force to be reckoned with as I spend Your love and encouragement wherever You place me, so the world will know the Savior who truly loves them unconditionally! In Jesus' name, Amen!

THOUGHTS FROM THE HEART:

Read James 1:25; 2:8-9, 12-13. James refers to the *"perfect law that gives freedom,"* he also calls it the *"royal law."* Describe in your own words the law he is referring to.

_____

_____

_____

In Matthew 22:36-40 Jesus makes a distinction between the heart, soul and mind; clearly these are three different battlefronts that must be conquered. (Note that the heart is number one.) Describe in your own words the difference between the three and why do you think the heart is mentioned first?

_____

_____

_____

_____

_____

Find four verses in the Bible that instruct believers to be encouragers. After each verse explain how that applies in our every day life.

_____

_____

_____

_____

SMALL GROUP DISCUSSION QUESTIONS:

Why does it take maturity and courage to be an encourager? Why is encouragement the apex of our faith?

_____

_____

_____

_____

_____

_____

What is necessary for our hearts to be made whole and healthy?

_____

_____

_____

_____

_____

Now that you have completed the study on *From Your Head To Your Heart*, share with your group how this book/study has impacted your life.

_____

_____

_____

_____

THOUGHTS:

NOTES

Introduction

1. As quoted in Mark C. Crowley, *Lead From the Heart: Transformational Leadership for the 21st Century* (Bloomington, IN: Balboa Press, 2011), 41.
2. Dr. Caroline Leaf, "The Three Brains," http://drleaf.com/about/scientific-philosophy/ (accessed October 7, 2014).

Chapter 2 – We Need A Brain Wash

1. Richard Shears, "Do Hearts Have Memories? Transplant Patient Gets Craving for Food Eaten by Organ Donor," Mail Online, December 23, 2009, http://www.dailymail.co.uk/news/article-1237998/Heart-transplant-patient-gets-craving-food-eaten-organ-donor.html (accessed October 15, 2014).
2. *World Book Encyclopedia*, vol. 8 (Chicago, IL: World Book Inc., 1989), s.v "grasshoppers."
3. Ibid.

Chapter 7 – Heart Attacks

1. As told by Ed Gungor in *Religiously Transmitted Diseases* (Nashville, TN: Thomas Nelson, 2006), 214. See also Lawrence O. Richards, *The Expository Dictionary of Bible Words* (Grand Rapids, MI: Zondervan, 1984) and *Spirit-Filled Life Bible NKJV* (Nashville, TN: Thomas Nelson, 1991), footnote on 1549.

Chapter 8 – Complexes . . . Will They Ever Go Away?

1. Peter J. Blackburn, "Dwight L Moody," Heroes of the Faith, 1999, http://peterjblackburn.net/people/moody.htm (accessed October 15, 2014).
2. Elizabeth Ruth Skoglund, *Bright Days, Dark Nights: With Charles Spurgeon in Triumph Over Emotional Pain* (Grand Rapids, MI: Baker Books, 2000).

Chapter 9 — There Is Treasure In The Trash

1. As quoted in L. B. Cowman, *Streams in the Desert* (Grand Rapids, MI: Zondervan, 1997), "August 13," 309.

Chapter 10 — All Access

1. *Strong's Greek Lexicon*, G4318, s.v. "*prosagōgē*," Blue Letter Bible, http://www.blueletterbible.org/lang/Lexicon/Lexicon.cfm?Strongs=G4318&t=KJV (accessed October 7, 2014).
2. *Strong's Greek Lexicon*, G3954, s.v. "*parrēsia*," Blue Letter Bible, http://www.blueletterbible.org/lang/Lexicon/Lexicon.cfm?Strongs=G3954 &t=KJV (accessed October 7, 2014).

ABOUT THE AUTHOR

Maria Durso is living proof that if anyone is in Christ, he is a new creation (2 Corinthians 5:17). Having come from a childhood devastated by loss and abuse she grew up thinking she could mask her pain with drugs. Her lifestyle could have left her hopeless and alone—yet God kept and preserved Maria's life.

Understanding firsthand the effects of abandonment, loneliness and rejection, she ministers to those whose hurt lies deep in the heart and works to minister to those who need hope. Armed with discernment, insight into the true character of God, honest about her own experience, and down to earth, Maria is an intercessor, teacher, and powerful speaker.

In 1975, immediately following the first most important walk Maria would ever take down a church aisle—Maria took her second most important walk down the aisle and married her life-long love, Michael Durso. Together she has pastored along side of her husband, Senior Pastor Michael Durso at Christ Tabernacle, the first church to be birthed from The Brooklyn Tabernacle, since 1985. They have witnessed, firsthand, the faithfulness and grace of God who supplies the needs of a continually growing urban church.

Believing that our greatest ministry is prayer, she oversees the Prayer Band, a group that intercedes daily for the needs of the congregation, various ministries, the Pastoral staff and requests that are phoned in to the church. Maria also oversees the Women's Ministry at Christ Tabernacle, a ministry that encourages women through fellowship, worship, and the Word of God.

Maria recently published her first book, *From Your Head to Your Heart*. With powerful examples from the Bible and redeeming stories from her testimony involving abandonment, loneliness, rejection, and drug use—this book will give you the keys to access the power in God's Word. Begin the renewing journey from your head to your heart today.

Blessed with a wonderful husband and three sons in ministry, their wives and grandmother to eight, Maria considers herself wholly blessed. The Durso's look forward to the great plans God has for their ministry, their lives, and their family.

God continues to open doors for her to minister in conferences, seminars, and retreats. Connect with Maria Durso at MariaDurso.com.

Made in the USA
Columbia, SC
22 August 2018